HACK PROOF
A Guide to Cybersecurity for Your Business

Sergey Poltev

Lucky Book Publishing

Published by Lucky Book Publishing:
www.luckybookpublishing.com

Paperback ISBN: 978-1-998287-14-7
Hardcover ISBN: 978-1-998287-15-4
E-book ISBN: 978-1-998287-13-0

1st edition, June 2024.

Praise for HACK PROOF

A Guide to Cybersecurity for Your Business

"An indispensable guide for any business owner navigating the treacherous waters of the digital age. This book demystifies cybersecurity, making it accessible and actionable for businesses of all sizes. Stay safe - A highly recommended read."

- George Weber, Chair of the Board of Directors, Calian Group Limited

"Sergey is a champion of empowering businesses of all sizes to protect themselves from modern cyber attacks. This book is a true testament to his dedication to helping the underdogs equip themselves with the critical information they need on their cybersecurity journey."

- Matthew Holland, Founder and CEO, Field Effect

"HACK PROOF offers practical, actionable steps for medium-sized businesses to enhance their cybersecurity without overwhelming resources. With a valuable self-assessment quiz and straightforward advice, it's perfect for business owners and IT leaders aiming to secure their companies efficiently and effectively."

- Carolann Jacobs, CISSP, CISM, CCSP, GCTI, Cybersecurity Expert

Sergey's passion for helping people and deep understanding of technology shine through on every page, inspiring my renewed dedication to advancing cybersecurity practices.

- Mark Tse, Cybersecurity Ambassador, Co-founder, Canadian Cyber Forum

"This book stands out for its ability to break down complex cybersecurity concepts into understandable and implementable steps. It's not just a book; it's a roadmap to safer business operations in the digital world."

- Dr. Bill Pomfret, MSc, FIOSH, RSP, FRSH; CEO, Safety Projects International Inc.

HACK PROOF book is a masterclass in cybersecurity, written with the insight only a seasoned professional could offer. Sergey's passion for both cybersecurity and business success shines through every page."

- Zachary Kitchen, Author of 'Compliance Formula', reformed hacker

"I have flown to a couple events around the country to have an opportunity to pick Sergey's brain on ways to help keep my own clients protected. When in Nashville, TN I was fortunate enough to see him on stage speaking about great service delivery options to serve his clients and immediately went back to Wisconsin and started implementing those changes. A true asset to any company fortunate enough to partner with him!"

- Rod Holum, Author, Speaker, CEO, Buttkicker of Cyber Criminals and Evangelist of AI

"With clarity and expertise, this book addresses the critical importance of cybersecurity for businesses today. It's packed with actionable insights and strategies that can be implemented immediately. A game-changer in the field."

- Leia Kupris Shilobod, CCP, CISM, Chief Security Officer, CompliancyIT

HACK PROOF is a must-read for anyone who knows they need to get started on cybersecurity but have yet to. The practical tips and straightforward advice will give you the confidence to strengthen your cybersecurity defenses. Highly recommended!"

- Matt Edwards, CISO

"A comprehensive, insightful, and utterly essential guide for today's business leaders. This book tackles the most pressing cybersecurity challenges with practical solutions. A pivotal read for securing your digital future."

– Stanislav Savchenko, CISA, CISSP, Senior IT Auditor at Export Development Canada

"From the first page to the last, this book is a treasure trove of invaluable information. It addresses the cybersecurity needs of businesses with precision and practicality. An essential addition to any business leader's library."

– Bharat Rudra, Co-founder and President of TiE Ottawa

If there was a how-to kit when you start a business, this book would be in it! In just a weekend, you'll transform your approach to cybersecurity with Sergey's deeply personal and insightful book. His firsthand experiences in cyber crime and defense bring a depth of authenticity and expertise to this essential read. His true-life stories of battling cybercrime make the learning process feel like an adventure. This is the go-to guide for any small business owner looking to boost their cyber defenses.

- Michael Bakaic, CEO & Founder, Iceberg Cyber

"There are only two types of companies: Those that have been hacked and those that don't know they've been hacked."

– Robert S. Mueller, III,
Former Director of the FBI and now Special Counsel into the Russian interference of the USA election

MY GIFT TO YOU!

I am so glad you're here!

As my Gift to you, get FREE Access to the Audiobook of HACK PROOF and other Free Resources by scanning the QR Code below or visiting HackProofBook.com

---

CONTENTS

INTRODUCTION

This book is for the entrepreneurs, the business owners, the IT professionals, and anyone who seeks to understand the digital threats we face and how to guard against them. Whether you are new to cybersecurity or looking to strengthen your existing knowledge, I hope this book serves as a valuable tool in your arsenal.

To make your exploration and understanding of this complex world a little easier, the book is divided into two parts.

Part One: Cracking the Code - Understanding Cybersecurity Threats.

The first five chapters cover how prevalent cyberthreats are today; why being "small" does not mean you are safe from attack; and how to create a cybersecurity culture to mitigate risk.

By learning from history, you will be able to use education and awareness, so history does not have to repeat itself.

We will show you how your false sense of security could lead to loss of reputation as well as income and profit.

And lastly, how vulnerable your network is to attack when it is not cybersecure.

However, it is one thing to understand and know the hacker industry and another thing altogether to know how to defend and secure your business. Now that you know what you are facing, the rest of the book is dedicated to showing you all the steps you need to be as hack proof as possible.

In Part Two - How to Hack Proof Your Business. You will find specific instructions and best practices to help protect your network and your business and keep your systems safe and secure. you will learn the most important ways and means to protect your business. Including:

Understanding cloud computing, what it is and how to have better security in a cloud environment.

- How to prevent Identity Theft from happening to you
- Staying secure while working from home

There are live case studies throughout the book that illustrate the impact of when security systems fail, and success stories of businesses that now thrive by being hack proof.

To wrap up your journey through HACK PROOF - A Guide to Cybersecurity for Your Business we have developed a concise self-assessment questionnaire. This tool is designed to provide you with a snapshot of your current cybersecurity posture and identify areas for improvement.

In the Appendices you will find:

- A comprehensive glossary of technical terms in plain English that will enable you to process the information you need and to be able to explain to IT teams when you have issues.
- The Q's and A's you may want to ask and find answers for in one place.

Dealing with IT issues is a major headache for most small businesses. Everything is integrated today because everything is online. Most people have neither the time nor the expertise to navigate that. As businesses grow and evolve, they often end up with a patchwork of IT systems from different vendors. Then, when something goes wrong, there's a lot of finger-pointing among the providers. Needless to say, this can be extremely frustrating for business owners.

But technology problems aren't just about a slow network or outdated software. Time and again, we've seen businesses waste far too much time doing things manually when there may be an easy IT solution. The problem is that most IT vendors are very narrowly focused.

Here's Why I Get You

I get it. Technology can be frustrating at times for businesses like yours - okay, maybe most of the time. But it's a necessary evil for you to stay competitive. To stay relevant, you've got to stay safe. Sometimes it just takes a push to kick you out of your comfort zone so you can start thinking about the future of your business.

I know a little something about needing a push.

As a kid growing up in a small Russian town overrun by the Mafia, I was forced to grow up way too fast. When I was just 10 years old, my father was unexpectedly killed in a car accident. I remember peering over his coffin and seeing my dad's body in that unnatural state. Right then and there, I knew my life would never be the same.

With my dad gone, it was now my responsibility to become the man of the house. I took on the role of being the protector of my family for my mom and my 2 siblings. Rather than just being a kid, I was constantly wondering how I could provide for my family.

I was 12 when my school visited our local library. My eyes lit up when I saw my very first personal computer At age 12, I finally KNEW how I could help provide for my widowed mother. After a school trip to the local library, my eyes lit up as I saw my very first personal computer. To me, it was a magical device that held the power to change all of our lives.

Seeing my passion for computers, my mom sacrificed and saved half her salary for six full months to buy me my first computer. I'll never forget the man who set up my computer. He told me how this device would allow me to learn anything I wanted and to communicate with anyone in the entire world. He was my superhero. And with that computer, he handed his superpowers over to me!

Like an unquenchable thirst, I was immediately obsessed with computers and technology. Ralph Waldo Emerson said, "For everything you have missed, you have gained something else." While losing my dad was the hardest time in my life, it opened up a world where I could help others by doing what I loved.

Rather than follow my friends' footsteps and use computers for games, I saw computers as a way to provide for my family. An entrepreneur at heart, at just 18 years old, I opened a gaming and internet café complete with over a dozen computers. I built each computer by hand, installed the software and connected them all to the internet. Back then, none of this was easy.

Word spread and my gaming café became very popular among the local teens. But in Russia, while successful businesses attract the public... they also attract the Mafia.

The Russian Mafia came into my business one evening and demanded money, as they put it, they wanted a cut so they could protect us. All I could think of was protecting my family, my employees, and my business. I looked them in the eyes and told them, 'No!'

Well, the Russian Mafia doesn't take kindly to being told "No." One of the Mafia picked up a baseball bat and SMASHED one of my expensive monitors. Then they threatened, "If we come back and you refuse to pay again, we will break ALL of your monitors." Running a business in Russia was challenging.

Too challenging.

"Growing up on American movies, I knew their technology was far more advanced. It was the land of opportunity, so I moved to North America to pursue my passion!"

With a Computer Science degree and only $500 in my pocket, I moved to Ottawa, Canada. Fortunately, I also packed a truckload of ambition, hard work and passion. I started my own IT company. Without fear of the Russian Mafia knocking at my door, I started to earn money. One of my personal values is "family comes first". As soon as that money came in, I would send it back home to my mom.

Those Mafia threats on Russian soil, to my business and my person happened in 2002. Today, my 25-person team and I are STILL fighting Russian criminals.

But this time, they pose massive cyber threats to small businesses everywhere. From ransomware to malware and phishing attacks to stolen data and identity theft, nearly 33 BILLION accounts will be breached this year costing businesses $8 TRILLION!

This is why I am the CEO of a Cybersecurity firm determined to protect small businesses from everyday massive cyber threats.

This book is the culmination of lessons learned, written so that you can rest easy at night. The comprehensive tools and strategies within these pages will help you be protected from both external and internal threats before they wreak havoc on your business.

Are you ready to start your journey to being HACK PROOF in your business?

Let's go!

- Sergey

PART 1

Cracking the Code - Understanding Cybersecurity Threats

CHAPTER 1

Keeping Your Small Business Secure

Key Takeaway: **This chapter covers how prevalent cyberthreats are today; why being "small" does not mean you are safe from attack; and how to create a cybersecurity culture to mitigate risk.**

Cybersecurity Risk Is Real For Small Businesses

Data breaches and cybersecurity attacks are a real concern for small businesses. Today, it's nearly impossible to count the number of attacks. Why? Because most cybercrimes get swept under the rug. Businesses would rather their clients or investors not know what happened than risk losing their trust and their business.

As the owner or manager of a small business, you've invested in a lot of physical assets. From your facility to equipment, you've put countless dollars into making sure you and your team have what it takes to ensure your work gets completed on budget and on time. And if you didn't protect your assets, it would leave your company unproductive and uncompetitive.

But what about your technology assets? Your computers, servers, printers, tablets, software programs and CRM all keep your business running efficiently. They also generate and store a lot of data, like client information, your employees' social security and bank details, inventory, profit and loss statements and other confidential information. A data breach could throw your business into turmoil, cost you clients and damage your reputation. If you haven't given the protection of your digital property serious consideration, you aren't the only small business that hasn't.

However, as small businesses continue to shrink the technology gap and take their place in line with larger companies, the opportunities for cyber-attackers to take advantage of your newly found status is VERY REAL.

I Can Tell You, No Target Is Too Small

It worries me when I hear small business owners say they're too "small potatoes" for hackers to bother with. The fact is, 43% of cyber-attacks happen to small businesses. And do you know why? Because only 14% were prepared to defend themselves. These attacks aren't harmless - or cheap. The average cost to a small business like yours is $200,000. That's enough to close your doors or make a hefty dent in your profit margin. You should make no mistake. Cyber-attacks don't just happen to big enterprises.

Ask For Enterprise-Level Solutions That Fit Your Budget

Do you know that your small business is wide open to the same security threats that big businesses face? While big businesses may face security threats on a larger scale, your small business is wide open to the same risks, like hacking, email phishing, malware and other nefarious Internet threats. And yet, some IT providers still don't take the needs of smaller companies seriously. They either offer "watered-down" versions of their solutions based on a client's budget or ignore them altogether. This attitude forces many firms like yours to manage cybersecurity in-house by someone who isn't an expert, exposing you to risk. I disagree with their approach. And so should you.

You may not have the budget of larger corporations, or the internal IT personnel to fight off today's hackers, but CapitalTek does. I make it my mission to "go to bat" for small and medium-sized businesses like yours, bringing you right-sized solutions that provide the protection you need. And no IT team on the payroll is needed.

Is it time to take cybersecurity seriously? Yes!

So, with the skyrocketing increase in cybersecurity risks, why aren't more small businesses taking it seriously? In my experience, it's not that they aren't taking it seriously, they just aren't sure how to take it seriously. Here's what I mean by that. They install basic (or even FREE) antivirus software on their computers and "set it and forget it." I see the appeal. Free is a great price tag. But the fact is, threats are more sophisticated today, and hackers are doing their homework. You can expect that as soon as a provider updates their free virus protection software, cybercriminals have already figured out how to get around it.

Creating A Cybersecurity Culture

Every managed services provider has a cybersecurity solution. I can guarantee you that every one of them has a different approach. That's not a good or bad thing. It's just different, which probably makes you scratch your head and wonder which one you should choose. I'll get to that in a minute. First, there is something YOU can and MUST do to protect your company from cyberthreats: make cybersecurity an ingrained part of your company culture.

Your employees are your first line of defense when it comes to protecting your business from cyberthreats. Cyber-attackers think of your employees as their unwitting partners in crime. Employees hand over credentials when they fall for a phishing scam or click an unknown link or download a file, allowing these bad actors to "come on in" without ever realizing that it's malicious.

Without hesitation, I can tell you that the most important step in combating cyber-attacks is weaving cybersecurity into your company's culture. Keeping your team informed of the do's and don'ts of online behavior is the first crucial step.

If we're being honest, most of us have probably said, "I'm too smart to fall for a phishing scam." Or "I can spot a suspicious email link a mile away." Or what about "I would never download something if I didn't know where it came from." This little lie we tell ourselves is also one reason why many small businesses like yours don't invest in cybersecurity in the first place – because no one in the organization does these things. I'm here to tell you that it does happen. And if it hasn't happened in your company yet, it will. Half of employees admit to opening emails they considered suspicious. So, how do you stop it before it's too late?

First, train your employees on the very REAL risk of cyberthreats. Teach them how to identify phishing emails. Remind them not to send passwords or other sensitive or personal identifying information in emails. Tell them to only open a file attachment if it's something they are expecting or if it's relevant to the work they're doing. Next, develop clear cybersecurity company policies with guidance on creating strong passwords and how often they need to change them. Set rules on using company devices for personal use. Finally, put somebody in charge of security. Which brings us back to the question: which cybersecurity solution is right for you?

It's important to know that cybersecurity isn't just a single software app or a one time service. Your best defense is a layered strategy that includes a combination of software, training, monitoring, hardware optimization and on-premise and cloud-based network security solutions. It takes just one gap in security for a hacker to get his foot in the door and burn the house down.

HACK PROOF TIP

Regularly schedule comprehensive security audits to evaluate the effectiveness of your cybersecurity measures. These audits should be conducted by external security experts who can provide an unbiased view of your security landscape. They will identify vulnerabilities in your network, suggest improvements, and help ensure compliance with industry standards and regulations.

Ready To Protect Your Small Business From Cybercriminals? We Can Help

We all have a comfort zone that we're happy to stay inside of. Until we're not. I hope you see this resource as the push you need to move forward in your cybersecurity plan. I can see you going back to this book often for ideas, strategies and solutions that are intended to help you and your team foster a cybersecurity culture against the bad guys of the Internet. I assure you, effective cybersecurity ain't easy! But if you use this resource as a starting point, you're on the right path.

CHAPTER 2

Why Cybercrime Today Can't Be Ignored

Key Takeaway: **This chapter covers why cybercrime cannot be ignored; defining cybercrime and reviewing the history; the escalating sophistication of criminals and the rising costs involved.**

Your business is growing. Sales are strong. Customers are happy. Operations are a well-oiled machine. Employee morale and productivity are off the charts. Then you start getting whispers from your team about some malware that your marketing guy unintentionally opened. "No worries," you think to yourself. "We should be protected since we bought that virus protection way back when."

You send your best computer guy to remedy the problem. Rebooting the computer does nothing. An assortment of virus removal tools comes up empty. Then he breaks it to you: "This isn't just a virus. It's ransomware. Sir, some hacker has access to all of our customers' files, and he locked them. He won't give us access unless we pay him $7,500... per account!"

Blood races to your head. You feel your heart pounding. Time stands still. This business you've invested all your time and money in has come to a grinding halt. And all of the customers you have relationships with – their files are at the mercy of an evil hacker who could be halfway around the world.

As a proud businessperson, you refuse to give in to these cybercriminals. You don't pay the ransom because it would bankrupt your business. Over the next few days and weeks, the results of this single event cripple your business. First, production and sales fall off a cliff. Second, since you're required by law to inform your customers their private information and credit cards are now compromised, you make those difficult calls... and consequently lose half of your clients. Next come the lawsuits and the fines. Finally, the public relations nightmare buries what's left of your business.

I know this probably sounds like hyperbole, like nothing that extreme could happen to a business like yours. Unfortunately, similar cybercrimes are becoming more and more common today. And no matter how protected you think your IT network is, these professional hackers and cybercriminals invest countless hours to always be one step ahead of you.

Cybercrime today can't be ignored. In fact, the more educated you are regarding the many facets of cybercrime today and the cyber security measures you need to implement to keep your network safe, the more confident you'll be to never face a nightmare scenario where you risk losing productivity, sales, customers, money and ultimately your business. So, let's start at the beginning...

What Exactly is Cybercrime?

Cybercrime is defined as any criminal activity that involves a computer, networked device or network. Cybercriminals, also called hackers, create malware, computer viruses and Trojan programs designed to wreak havoc on computers and networks around the world. At the very least, these cybercrimes can slow the speed of the computers on your network. At the other extreme, their actions can significantly disrupt and even cripple a business.

There are multiple categories of cybercrime, but all of them begin with a computer virus or malware program. These cybercriminals utilize these subversive and often undetected viruses to achieve their specific criminal objectives, which are usually:

- Stealing usernames, passwords, bank accounts or private information
- Accessing and selling personal information or

confidential business information

- Advertising products or services on victims' computers
- Infecting computers or a network to run spam campaigns, distributed denial-of-service attacks (DDoS attacks) and/or blackmailing operations to force a substantial payment

While the motive of some cybercriminals is to directly damage or disable computers, devices and entire networks, most cybercriminals are in it for the money. Profit-driven criminal activity can include ransomware attacks, e-mail and Internet fraud, identify theft and attempts to steal financial accounts, credit cards or other payment information. Today, many cybercriminals are targeting corporate data for both theft and resale.

We tend to think of cybercriminals as men cloaked in hoodies conducting their malfeasance on the dark web. That's not always the case. Many are dressed in suits and work in a corporate office, just like well-respected businesspeople. Also, rather than hiding via the dark web, they are doing their damage in more public channels, such as social media.

History of Cybercrime

While the Internet certainly enabled cybercrime to become more prevalent, the first instances of cybercrime were committed before the Internet as we know it today existed. In the 1970s, before computers were in households, cybercrime occurred over telephones. "Phone phreaking" was the practice of exploiting hardware and frequency vulnerabilities in a telephone network to get free or reduced phone rates.

The advent of email in the late '80s marked the first major wave of cybercrime. Do you remember the Nigerian Prince scam? Of course, phishing scams like those required a total buy-in from the recipient and involved physically sending money. As a result, similar email scams only conned those who were ill-informed and desperate.

With the advancement of web browsers in the 1990s, we saw the proliferation of viruses in this next wave of cybercrime. Back then, viruses lived on questionable websites. Simply the act of visiting those websites brought about uninvited problems to your computer. Perhaps your computer ran slower. Maybe you had to endure annoying pop-up ads on your screen. Perhaps you were redirected to a porn site or two, which made for some explaining to your colleagues or spouse. All in all, while these viruses seemed serious at the time, they are almost laughable compared to what viruses can do today.

In the year 2000, America first learned of the word "malware." The infamous ILOVEYOU worm infected 50 million computers by accessing their private email contacts and corrupting data. Before the ILOVEYOU worm, viruses and malware were easy to spot: if you don't know the sender or the message looks sketchy, don't open it and certainly don't click on it. That single piece of malware changed the rules. Suddenly, even trusted sources with seemingly innocent messages had to be scrutinized. Fortunately, this sparked a surge of antivirus software.

In the early 2000s, social media came to life. What could possibly go wrong when you have practically the whole world putting their private information online? You guessed it: identity theft and stealing personal information. These online hackers stole personal information to access bank accounts, set up credit cards or commit other financial fraud.

Today, we have crossed the line to a far more aggressive and more damaging brand of cybercrime. One where it's a global criminal industry totaling nearly half a trillion dollars annually. These cybercriminals operate in gangs, use well-established methods and target anyone who is connected to the Internet. And while the tools to detect and divert these cybercrimes are getting far more sophisticated, so are the cybercriminals today.

Sobering Cybercrime Statistics

No matter how many news stories you see about

cybercrime attacks, no matter how many businesses you personally know that have been compromised, you can only get a crystal-clear picture of this massive industry (yes, cybercrime is an industry) when you see the statistics.

First, cybercrime represents the fastest-growing type of crime in the world. Cyberattacks are not only growing exponentially in frequency and total dollar theft, but they are also increasing in size, scope and sophistication. Make no mistake, business is booming for cybercriminals.

The Cost of Cybercrime

- Cybercrime was predicted to cost the world approximately $8 trillion in 2023. This figure is expected to grow by 15 percent per year over the next few years, showcasing a significant increase in the economic impact of cybercrime.
- The global cost of cybercrime is forecasted to jump to $23.84 trillion by 2027, a substantial rise from $8.44 trillion in 2022. This underscores the escalating challenge and financial impact of cyber threats worldwide.

Cybercrime Is Commonplace Today

- Hackers attack every 39 seconds. That's 2,244 times

a day on average.

- The FBI receives an average of 900 cybercrime-related complaints a day – that's over 300,000 a year!
- 85% of organizations today report experiencing phishing and social engineering attacks.
- 68% of business leaders believe their cyber security risks are increasing.
- Cybercrime is more prevalent in the US than in any other country.

Most Organizations Are Ill-Prepared Against Cyberattacks

- 64% of Americans have never even checked to see if they were affected by a data breach.
- 56% of Americans don't know what steps to take in the event of a data breach.
- It takes organizations 206 days on average to identify a breach. Then, it takes a total of 314 days to contain the breach.
- Over 50% of devices that got infected once were reinfected within that same year.

Where Is Cybercrime Headed?

While proactive IT services providers using today's

latest software and technologies can keep many of the viruses, malware and ransomware off of networks and computers, cybercriminals and hackers are also becoming increasingly sophisticated. In the next few years, we can expect to experience more aggressive cyberattacks that are far more difficult to detect.

What does this mean for you?

Without shielding your business, your data and your money with the right IT experts and tools you are at great risk.

While nobody can pinpoint exactly where cybercriminals will hit next, we have a few likely targets.

Hacking the Internet of Thing

The Internet is no longer confined to our computers. It's everywhere. From our cars to our smart home devices, like Alexa and Echo, to our security systems and appliances, to our watches and fitness trackers, this proliferation of the Internet is referred to as the Internet of Things (IoT). And as the Internet spreads, so do the cyberattacks and viruses

These convenient devices are usually wirelessly connected to the Internet, which makes them even more vulnerable. In the near future, hackers will find ways to control entire systems all from a single compromised entry point. Just imagine the widespread ramifications when your wireless camera hacks a thermostat that connects to a power plant.

> **HACK PROOF TIP**
>
> The more smart devices you have in your home or your office, the more gateways you have into your entire network

Social Engineering

As we become more and more protective of our private information, cybercriminals are becoming smarter and using more sophisticated technologies to make us let our guard down. Social engineering is how they will accomplish this in the future. It will be the new norm in hacking.

Social engineering occurs when organized cybercriminals know every possible detail about their targets. They know when their targets post on Facebook, which colleagues' emails they open and which websites they visit. With that critical information, these more advanced hackers can pose as an employee, friend or loved one. When that happens, it's no longer an email from a Nigerian Prince that's easily detected and deleted. Now it's an email from your boss or business partner to get your passwords or financial details. Make no mistake, in the near future, you'll always need to keep your guard up.

> **HACK PROOF TIP**
>
> Strengthen your defenses against sophisticated social engineering attacks by enhancing your email authentication protocols. Talk to your IT consultant and ask about advanced email security measures such as DMARC (Domain-based Message Authentication, Reporting, and Conformance), SPF (Sender Policy Framework), and DKIM (DomainKeys Identified Mail). These technologies help prevent impersonators from spoofing emails that appear to come from trusted sources within your organization.

Cloud Attacks

Over the last few years, businesses have been racing to the cloud. Using cloud-based solutions, businesses have been able to increase their operational efficiencies while minimizing costs. Operating in the cloud does provide another layer of security. However, since the majority of companies now keep much of their valuable data in the cloud, cybercriminals are working overtime to find a way into these mines of data.

Widespread Ransomware

Just like all of us, cybercriminals want to be paid. They've realized one of today's most lucrative cybercrimes involves stealing and locking down companies' private data for the purpose of collecting a ransom. Ransomware is a malware that infects computers and limits access to files until a hefty ransom has been paid.

- Ransomware continues to be a major threat, with a significant increase in the number and severity of attacks. In 2022, 73% of businesses experienced a ransomware attack, highlighting the pervasive risk across industries.
- The global cost of ransomware is expected to exceed $30 billion in 2023. This figure underscores the substantial financial impact ransomware attacks have on businesses worldwide.
- The average ransom demanded by attackers has risen sharply, with figures reaching up to $1.5 million in 2023. This indicates the increasing boldness and sophistication of cybercriminals in their ransom demands.
- Looking ahead, global ransomware damage costs are predicted to skyrocket, reaching $265 billion by 2031. This projection is based on the expectation that ransomware will become the fastest-growing type of cybercrime, with a business, consumer, or device falling victim every 2 seconds by 2031.

After reviewing how cybercrime could bring your business operations, productivity and sales to a screeching halt; how cyberattacks could cost you considerable money in fines, lawsuits, sales and even ransom; and after reading through the sobering statistics about how cybercrime has impacted businesses around the globe, you will have a clearer picture of the future of cyberattacks and you realize the serious nature of cybercrime and how you must take action now to mitigate your risks.

In the next chapter, you'll get a peek into some of the largest data breaches in the world and how they cost businesses considerably in terms of finances, customers and reputation.

CHAPTER 3

The Largest Data Breaches of the 21st Century

Key Takeaway: This chapter provides an overview of the largest breaches to date; using education and awareness so history does not have to repeat itself.

Data breaches happen just about every hour of every day. Far too many fly under the radar because most of them involve small businesses. While they turn business owners' and employees' lives upside down, you'll rarely learn about those cybercrimes on the news or on social media.

The cyberattacks that are in the spotlight involve giant brands we know and cost millions of dollars in theft and damages. The following case studies highlight how large companies were breached, what data was compromised, the financial and customer-loss fallout and how their management teams handled the situation. From these true stories, you can glean lessons of what to do to better protect your business from cybercrime and the steps you should take after a cyberattack.

Heartland Payment Systems

Heartland Payment Systems is a credit card processing company that started in 1997. When you're entrusted by your clients to handle their customers' credit cards as well as mobile payments, payroll and loyalty cards, cyber security should be job one. Because if all of the credit card information that they process gets into the wrong hands, it could mean untold millions in damages.

Well, that very nightmare happened in 2008 when Heartland Payment Systems fell victim to one of the largest data security breaches in US history. Hackers attacked their systems and made off with the information from 100 million credit and debit cards!

Heartland Payment Systems was just one of several companies that the gang of hackers managed to break into using SQL injection attacks. They also stole from 7-Eleven and Hannaford Brothers.

In an effort to prove to its customers and vendors that they had tightened their cyber security, Heartland Payment Systems put out a promise:

"Heartland Payment Systems is so confident in the

security of its payment processing technology, that it announced a new breach warranty for its users. The warranty program will reimburse merchants for costs incurred from a data breach that involves the Heartland Secure credit card payment processing system."

Often, when a company gets hacked, there's a long line of vendors who also endure compromised data and financial fallout. Card-issuing banks such as American Express have had to pay the costs of reissuing cards. Many banks have sued Heartland Payment Systems to recover these unexpected costs.

While their warranty may provide a little comfort and goodwill to its customers and vendors, Heartland did take a monster- sized hit to its financials as a result of the data breach. They were forced to pay American Express $3.6 million to settle charges directly resulting from its compromised data. Heartland has since agreed to also pay out fines to Visa and MasterCard. They have set aside $12.6 million to handle charges related to the hack.

HACK PROOF TIP

Heartland Payment Systems' experience underscores the critical importance of having a robust incident response plan in place. Your business should develop a comprehensive plan that details every step to be taken in the event of a data breach, including immediate containment strategies, communication with affected parties, and remediation processes. Regularly update this plan to address new cybersecurity threats and ensure all team members are trained on their roles during an incident sources within your organization.

Adobe

Adobe, the creator of photo-editing and creative software, was hacked in 2013 when a cyberattack exposed Adobe customer IDs as well as encrypted passwords and credit card records. As bad as the attack was, Adobe made it worse by severely underestimating the total number of affected accounts.

Initially, Adobe said hackers had gained access to encrypted credit card records and login information for about 2.9 million users. Weeks later, Adobe had to do an about-face when they revealed that a total of 38 million accounts were hacked – over 10 TIMES their initial estimate.

What exactly did the hackers do with the data they stole? According to a security blogger who first reported the breach, a file was uploaded to a hacking forum that contained millions of usernames and "hashed" passwords stolen from Adobe. When a password is hashed, it is converted into a string of characters that can't be reversed to reveal the original text.

In response to the cyberattack, Adobe took reactive measures, including resetting customer passwords on all compromised accounts, informing breached-account customers via e-mail and posting a security alert page on their website. Adobe was fined $1 million in a multistate lawsuit as a result of the incident.

eBay

EBay, Inc., the world's online marketplace, was hacked in 2014. Initially, the company didn't believe the security breach affected customer accounts and therefore kept the breach private. After forensic investigators took a closer look, eBay realized that hackers had accessed the personal data of ALL 145 million of its customers, ranking it as one of the largest cyberattacks on corporations.

Beyond the attack itself, eBay received a backlash from its customers and the media as a result of their improper handling of the incident. First, they were slow to investigate the data breach, and second, once they realized that customers' data was stolen, they didn't inform customers in an expeditious manner.

Hackers had used the credentials of three corporate employees, which eventually gave them access to the entire eBay user database. Once in the database, they were able to access both e-mail addresses and encrypted passwords belonging to all 145 million eBay users. While it took some time, e-mail notifications went out to all users, and their passwords had been reset.

Home Depot

In 2014, home improvement retailer Home Depot faced a massive public relations nightmare when hackers penetrated their network. By utilizing a vendor's stolen login credentials, these cybercriminals were able to install their own malware that stole customers' credit card data and e-mail addresses. Installed on the stores' self-checkout registers, this malware was able to evade even the latest antivirus software. Unfortunately, this data breach went undetected for several months.

All told, this cyber security attack resulted in information from 56 million credit cards and debit cards in the United States and Canada to be stolen. In addition, 53 million email addresses were compromised. Home Depot said that among the private information stolen were the customer's name, credit card number, expiration date and the three- or four-digit verification code on the back of the card.

Aside from costing Home Depot many millions of dollars in bad press and lost customers, the initial breach cost them $62 million. After incurring these costs and customer attrition, the Atlanta- based company agreed to pay $19.5 million to settle a class-action lawsuit brought by shoppers. This lawsuit included a $13 million fund to compensate customers for out-of-pocket expenses.

In addition to the class-action lawsuit, Home Depot gave many customers gift cards in the amount of $50 to show appreciation for being loyal. They also offered customers free identity-protection services, including a year of credit report monitoring. Finally, Home Depot has been forced to adopt new data security measures to protect its customers from future cyberattacks.

Yahoo

Having ONE BILLION of your customers' accounts hacked is historically bad. Finding out years later that it was actually THREE BILLION accounts – every single Yahoo user – is even worse. In 2013, Yahoo suffered an epic data breach when cybercriminals stole names, passwords and email addresses from its massive customer base. Fortunately, financial information was not compromised.

After an investigation with a third-party forensic

team in 2017, Yahoo obtained new intelligence and now believes that ALL user accounts were affected. Yes, three billion accounts in all!

Yahoo took action and sent emails to everyone affected. They also required password changes and invalidated unencrypted security questions, all in an effort to protect user information.

While it's not clear who was behind Yahoo's cyberattack, security analysts reported that the stolen data was being sold on the dark web, an underground version of the Internet that utilizes specific software and special authorizations to access.

To add fuel to the fire, hackers attacked Yahoo again a year later. This time, the cybercrime affected approximately 500 million customers. Just recently, the Department of Justice indicted two Russian spies and two hackers for that second attack.

MyFitnessPal

In 2018, Under Armour's popular nutrition and exercise app, MyFitnessPal, was hacked. This data breach impacted approximately 150 million users. There are a few things Under Armour did right in this case: first, by separating their users' data, the intrusion only exposed usernames, e-mail addresses and passwords. It could have been far worse if data such as credit card numbers, locations and birthdays were grabbed as well.

Second, they responded very quickly to the cybercrime. Too often it takes months or even years for businesses to even realize their data was hacked and compromised. Then, it takes even more weeks to internally investigate the matter and then come forward to their customers and the public. Under Armour realized the breach occurred in late February, discovered it in late March and went public with it less than a week later. That's surprisingly fast.

Uber

If there's ever a lesson into improperly handling a data breach, it's Uber. In November of 2016, the international ride- hailing company, Uber, had private information stolen from both riders and drivers. The hackers stole email addresses, names and cellphone numbers from 50 million riders and 7 million drivers. In addition, they stole about 600,000 driver's license numbers from drivers.

To make matters worse, the hackers demanded a ransom of $100,000 to not go public about the breach. Uber agreed to pay the hackers $100,000 in an effort to keep the incident quiet. In an embarrassing lack of transparency, Uber hid this data breach from its drivers and riders for over a year!

The Uber breach settlement is one of the largest in history for a data privacy case. The company agreed to pay $148 million in total, which will be distributed among all states involved. There are two reasons the penalty was so steep: first, they failed to provide timely notice of the breach. Each state's individual privacy laws require businesses to quickly disclose any data breach. Second, Uber engaged in deceptive trade practices. The state of Texas claimed that Uber violated their Deceptive Trade Practices Act by failing to provide adequate security after claiming their data was secured.

Marriott

In 2018 Marriott International disclosed a breach affecting 500 million guests of its Starwood hotel chain, involving personal data including names, phone numbers, email addresses, passport numbers, and travel information.

This breach stemmed from security vulnerabilities in the Starwood hotels' guest reservation system, which Marriott inherited when it acquired Starwood in 2016. Cybercriminals had gained unauthorized access to the system as early as 2014, utilizing remote access trojans (RATs) due to digital vulnerabilities like outdated Windows Server versions and open remote desktop protocol (RDP) ports. Despite these breaches occurring before and during the acquisition process, Marriott failed to conduct a detailed cybersecurity audit of Starwood's technology, which allowed the attackers to remain undetected for years. Marriott identified the breach in September 2018 following a security alert and disclosed it publicly in November 2018. The breach resulted in substantial recovery costs, reputational damage, and significant legal ramifications.

This incident underscores the importance of prioritizing cybersecurity during mergers and acquisitions, the risks of exposed RDP ports, the necessity of effective security and threat detection software, and the crucial role of adequate cyber insurance coverage.

HACK PROOF TIP

The Marriott International case illustrates the crucial need for comprehensive cybersecurity due diligence during the mergers and acquisitions (M&A) process. When acquiring another company, it is essential to conduct an extensive audit of their cybersecurity posture, including software, hardware, and network infrastructure. This should involve assessing the security of all integrated systems and ensuring that any known vulnerabilities are addressed before the acquisition is finalized.

Capital One

How much damage can a single hacker do to a giant financial enterprise? How about $150 million in damages. In 2019, a single cybercriminal was accused of breaking into Capital One's server and accessing more than 100 million customers' accounts and credit card applications.

This young woman, who previously worked as a software engineer for a tech company, gained access to 140,000 Social Security numbers, one million Canadian Social Insurance numbers and 80,000 bank accounts. In addition, she stole many customers' names, addresses, credit scores, credit limits, balances and more. By exploiting a misconfigured web application firewall, she was able to sneak into their network and access these customer records.

Perhaps the only reason Capital One realized they were hacked was because the cybercriminal took to social media and practically bragged about her theft. First, she posted on GitHub, a software development platform, about the information she stole from Capital One, including her full first, middle and last name. Next, she boasted on social media about her illegal score.

Finally, on a Slack chat service channel she explained exactly how she broke into Capital One's data files, claiming to use a special command to extract files in their directory, which was stored on Amazon's servers. She even wrote, "I wanna get it off my server that's why I'm archiving all of it lol." It wasn't long after her posts that the case was in the hands of the FBI.

Capital One notified people affected by the breach. In addition, they will make free credit monitoring and identity protection available to their customers. They expect to incur between $100 million and $150 million in costs related to the hack, including customer notifications, credit monitoring, technology costs, legal support and lost customers due to this cybercrime.

Twitter

In July 2020, Twitter (now X) faced a major cybersecurity breach that had significant implications. During this incident, 130 high-profile Twitter accounts were compromised by external parties in a coordinated social engineering attack. The perpetrators gained access to Twitter's administrative tools, allowing them to directly alter the accounts and post tweets. They used social engineering techniques to exploit Twitter employees and manipulate the system.

The scam tweets posted from these compromised accounts urged individuals to send bitcoin currency to a specific cryptocurrency wallet, promising that the money sent would be doubled and returned as a charitable gesture. Within minutes, more than 320 transactions took place, resulting in over US$110,000 worth of bitcoins deposited in one account before the scam messages were removed by Twitter.

Solarwinds

In a 2021 sophisticated cyberattack, SolarWinds, a software company, was breached, leading to the compromise of several U.S. government agencies and numerous corporations, impacting tens of thousands of SolarWinds' clients worldwide. The attackers managed to inject malicious code into the software's updates, which, when installed by SolarWinds customers, provided the attackers access to the victims' networks. This incident was notable not only for its scale and sophistication but also for the range of targets, including government agencies and private organizations.

This breach underscored the importance of robust cybersecurity practices, including timely application of security updates, comprehensive monitoring of network and system activities, and user education to defend against phishing and other social engineering attacks.

23andMe

In December 2023, DNA testing company 23andMe confirmed that hackers had stolen the ancestry data of half of its customers, some 7 million people. However, this admission came weeks after it was first revealed in October that user and genetic data had been taken after a hacker published a portion of the stolen profile and DNA information of 23andMe users on a well-known hacking forum.

23andMe initially said that hackers had accessed user accounts by using stolen user passwords that were already made public from other data breaches, but later admitted that the breach had also affected those who opted into its DNA Relatives feature, which matches users with their genetic relatives.

After revealing the full extent of the data breach, 23andMe changed its terms of service to make it more difficult for breach victims to file legal claims against the company. Lawyers described some of these changes as "cynical" and "self-serving." If the breach did one good thing, it's that it prompted other DNA and genetic testing companies to beef up their user account security in light of the 23andMe data breach.

AT&T

In March 2024, AT&T confirmed another significant data breach affecting over 70 million of its current and former customers, with sensitive information surfacing on the dark web. This incident involved the personal details of 7.6 million active and 65.4 million former account holders. The compromised data varied across individuals, potentially including social security numbers, full names, email and mailing addresses, phone numbers, birth dates, and AT&T account details, including passcodes.

As AT&T grapples with this breach, their immediate response has been to notify affected customers through data breach letters, emphasizing the severity of the cyber security incident. The company is offering free credit monitoring, identity theft detection, and resolution services, alongside an insurance policy covering up to $1 million in damages due to identity theft.

This breach is another in a series of cybersecurity challenges for AT&T, following a previous incident in March 2023 involving a third-party vendor that impacted 9 million wireless customers.

Because these global brands have tens of thousands of employees and hundreds of millions or more in revenue, their security breaches are magnified and made examples of. Their fines are massive and their customer fallout is often irreparable.

HACK PROOF CASE STUDY

John, Kitchen Remodeling - Ending Invoice Fraud

John's kitchen remodeling company, driven by 15 creative professionals, was hit by invoice fraud. Our solution included Intelligent Network Threat Alerting and 24/7 Network Traffic Analysis to monitor financial transactions, bolstered by a robust Password Manager. These measures eradicated the threat of fraud, restoring client trust and securing the company's financial integrity, allowing John and his team to focus on their passion for transforming homes acquisition is finalized.

But don't rest comfortably just yet. What you're about to read in the next chapter is the truth: small businesses like yours are cybercriminals' #1 target.

CHAPTER 4

Why YOU Are Cybercriminals' #1 Target

Key Takeaway: Busting major misconceptions; outlining the costs and risks if you are breached; how your false sense of security could lead to loss of reputation as well as income and profit.

CEOs and business owners of small businesses share many of the same beliefs about cybercriminals and the odds that their own businesses will be attacked. They have a FALSE sense of security. The reason: many of them buy into a number of misconceptions.

Misconception #1: Our business is too small. Cybercriminals are mainly targeting major corporations.

On the surface, that brand of thinking seems logical. After all, why would you target small businesses when these global giants have a ton more data and money to steal? Plus, you tend to only see headlines about cyberattacks involving major players like J.P. Morgan, Target, Experian, Home Depot and Yahoo.

That's exactly what cybercriminals are counting on you to believe. It makes small businesses easy prey because they tend to put zero protections in place or grossly inadequate ones.

Why don't you hear about banks being robbed anymore? Because criminals know that banks have incredibly sophisticated security measures in place. Not only is it very difficult to rob a bank, it's nearly impossible to get away with it and not get caught. Therefore, most criminals go after soft targets, such as homes or gas stations. This same logic is the reason most cybercriminals target small businesses and not the Fortune 500 businesses. They know you're not spending millions on cyber security and you don't have a massive IT team working 24/7 to protect your assets.

The National Cyber Security Alliance reports that one in five small businesses have been victims of cybercrime in the last year. Of course, that number includes only the ones that self-reported. Most small businesses are too embarrassed or afraid to report breaches because they don't want the PR nightmare. Also, while many countries have adopted the "you must report a security breach" mentality, business owners know there are no penalties or fines if they don't report. Of course, countries are now working on legislation to penalize those who do not self-report.

It's safe to assume far more small businesses have been hacked than the statistics show. And if you never implement stronger IT security measures, you are essentially a "sitting duck," just waiting for the inevitable to become another small business statistic.

HACK PROOF CASE STUDY

Tanya, Real Estate Law - Safeguarding Legal Documents

Tanya's real estate law firm, with 18 dedicated professionals, was threatened by ransomware. We responded by setting up Cloud Layer Detection and Response, introducing a DNS Firewall to prevent access to malicious sites, and implementing Continuous Dark Web Monitoring. These measures ensured their sensitive case files were shielded from digital threats, reinforcing the firm's commitment to client confidentiality and trust.

Misconception #2: We have competent IT people / We have adequate protections in place.

If you have an entire IT department or even one IT person, you may believe you already have a shield of protection around your computers, important files and network. But wouldn't you agree that your IT personnel and protections are nowhere close to the sophisticated security of eBay, Marriott, Equifax, Uber, Home Depot and Google?

In November of 2018, cyberthieves stole data from approximately 500 million Marriott International customers. These attackers first entered their network in 2014 and were not detected until four years later!

Equifax, one of the largest credit bureaus in the US, had a data breach that exposed 147.9 million customers. Even worse, 209,000 consumers had their credit card data compromised. Approximately 5 million usernames and passwords of Google Gmail account holders were compromised and leaked on a Russian forum site.

If these titans of industry that have the newest cyber security software and technologies and scores of cyber security experts can get hacked, so can small businesses like yours.

Risks to Your Business

Though you never imagine it could happen to your business, what could you realistically expect if you fall victim to a cybercrime? Fact is, even one event could trigger an avalanche of disruptions, costs and damages to your business that could last months or years, or worse, you may simply never recover and be forced to close your doors. Here's hoping you never have to endure the costly and time-consuming cleanup of a cyberattack. But if it happens to you and your business, the following are the dominoes you can expect to fall.

A Mountain of Costs

Just one breach, one ransomware attack or one rogue employee can create untold hours of extra work from your entire team. Then there's business interruption, downtime and backlogged work delivery for your current clients. Because business productivity slides and attention to prospects and existing clients suffer, it's not uncommon to see a drop in sales for several weeks or months.

Then come the costs associated with the hack. First, there are forensics costs to determine what kind of hack occurred, which parts of the network were affected and what data was compromised. Second, you can expect to pay for emergency IT restoration costs for getting back up and running, if that's even possible. Third, if the attack was ransomware, you'll be forced to pay the ransom and hope these criminals who hacked your network honor their word and give you your data back.

Hint:

Can you really trust criminals to be honest? You may pay and still not get your data back! The price may even go up! Then you can expect your cash flow will be significantly disrupted and budgets blown up. After all, when your customers' private information is stolen and you're begging them not to leave, do you really think marketing becomes a priority?

According to the Cost of Data Breach Study conducted by Ponemon Institute, the average cost of a data breach is $225 per compromised record. Think about how many records you have. Clients, employees, prospects. Now multiply that number by $225, and you'll start to get a sense of the costs to your organization. (Note: Health care data breach costs are the highest among all industries, and doctors can have thousands of patients.)

HACK PROOF TIP

Given the high cost of data breaches, as highlighted by the aforementioned study, it's crucial to implement strong encryption protocols for storing and transmitting sensitive data. Additionally, practice data minimization to reduce the volume of data at risk. Only collect and retain necessary information and ensure it is protected at all stages of its lifecycle. By encrypting data and minimizing the amount stored, you significantly reduce potential breach impacts and associated costs, safeguarding both your financial resources and your organization's reputation.

Government Fines, Legal Fees, Lawsuits

Beyond the loss of customers and sales, beyond the restoration costs and lack of productivity, if your business is the victim of a cyberattack, there are also massive external expenses you are likely to incur.

The government will be among the first in line with their hands in your pockets. Breach notification statutes remain one of the most active areas of the law. Right now, several senators are lobbying for "massive and mandatory" fines pertaining to data breaches and data privacy. Government couldn't care less that it was a criminal act and wasn't entirely your fault. They expect you to pay punitive fines.

If you're in the health care or financial services sectors, you have additional notification requirements under the Health Insurance Portability and Accountability Act (HIPAA), the Securities and Exchange Commission (SEC) and the Financial Industry Regulatory Authority (FINRA). Beyond simply notifying clients with compromised information, if the breach involves more than 500 clients or patients, you must notify a prominent media outlet about the incident. That's when a public relations firestorm is ignited, and clients leave in droves.

Then there are legal fees and the cost of legal counsel to help you respond to your clients and the media. Speaking of legal, in today's litigious society, you can fully expect some people whose private information was stolen (customers, vendors, employees) to sue your company. Proving your security was sufficient to protect their assets would probably be a losing battle. Therefore, you would most likely lose the lawsuit, costing you tens of thousands, hundreds of thousands or more. It adds up quickly.

Loss of Reputation and Customers

Your reputation IS your business. If you have a data breach and your customers' private information is stolen – whether it's their credit card numbers, their email addresses or their passwords – it is your responsibility to inform each and every compromised account. Ideally, you should let them know of the data breach through multiple forms of communication (e-mail, phone call, notice on your website) as quickly as possible so they have time to cancel their credit cards and change their passwords.

Nobody likes delivering news that will negatively affect their business, but it must be done. Yes, once your customers are aware their private information was compromised, you can expect some pretty harsh responses. Statistics show that 83% of consumers in the US claim they will stop spending at a business for several months after a security breach, and 21% will never return to that business. Even worse, lots of your customers will take to social media, YouTube and review-type websites like Yelp.com to express their anger and smear your company. Plus, the customers who believe they lost significant money or time may even consider legal action. The first wave of business loss comes from these disgruntled customers. The next wave of loss results from your damaged reputation. Once word spreads that you didn't have the security protections in place to keep your customers' private information safe, it's a black eye for your company's trustworthiness. People will steer clear of your business and run toward your competitors.

What's worse than a data breach, losing customers and the reputational fallout that follows? Not telling your customers at all and trying to cover it up. Companies like Yahoo and Uber are learning that lesson the hard way, facing multiple class- action lawsuits for not telling their users immediately when they discovered they were hacked. Nowadays, there are monitoring and forensics tools that can easily trace a data breach right back to the company where and when the breach occurred. In other words, there is nowhere to hide. Delay in reporting a breach snowballs the fines, lawsuits and customer backlash.

While a data breach that exposes your customers' trusted passwords, credit card numbers and personal information is bad, covering it up or simply pretending it never occurred could be the death of your business. Customers may forgive a mistake. They certainly won't forgive lying. And when word gets around that you cared more about protecting your profits than protecting your customers, it will take years to undo that damage.

HACK PROOF CASE STUDY

Fr Tom, Church - Preserving a Community's Trust

Fr Tom's church, a cornerstone of hope for its congregation supported by a dedicated team of 5, faced cyber vandalism. We safeguarded their online presence with Active Malware and APT Protection and Continuous Dark Web Monitoring, ensuring the church's message remained untainted. This preserved the sanctuary's digital and communal peace, allowing Fr Tom to continue spreading hope without the shadow of cyber threats.

Bank Fraud

Not all cybercriminals target your customers. Many of them will directly target you and your business. More than stealing information, they'll want to steal your money. There is a false assumption today that any money stolen by a cybercriminal is instantly and easily replaced by your bank or financial institution. This is NOT always the case.

If your bank account is accessed and funds stolen, the bank is not responsible for replacing those funds. Take the true story of successful author and CEO of Gazelles, Inc., Verne Harnish. Verne was using free, public WiFi while out of the country, which allowed hackers to gain access to his username and password so they could access his email account. The hackers, who are believed to be based in China, reviewed his sent emails to mimic the same verbiage Verne used before and then sent an e-mail to his assistant asking her to wire funds to three different locations. Because Harnish was involved with multiple real estate and investment ventures and because it looked just like previous requests to wire money, it didn't strike the assistant as out of the ordinary. Plus, how many people would question what their boss asked them to do?

The assistant responded in the affirmative, and the hackers, posing as her boss, assured her that it was to be done. The cybercriminals also deleted Verne's daily bank alerts so he wouldn't be tipped off when the money was stolen. All told, these cybercriminals stole $400,000. What's worse, the bank was not responsible and the money to this day has never been recovered.

How could you possibly prevent a similar theft or someone trying to access your credit or debit cards? You could set up both email AND text alerts for all financial transactions, including your credit and debit cards. Of course, you would need to thoroughly review each alert to ensure each transaction was legitimate.

False Sense of Security

Right now, you're probably thinking, "My assistant would never do that." But that's what everybody thinks: "Not my assistant. Not my employees. Not my company." Everybody thinks like this until it happens to them.

Do you honestly believe that your staff is incapable of making a single mistake or a poor judgment? Nobody believes they will be in a car wreck when they leave the house every day, but you still wear a seat belt. You don't expect a life-threatening crash, but that's not a valid reason to avoid buckling up. Unless you're equally protected in your business, you are at risk for losing considerable money, lots of customers and mountains of goodwill and reputation.

Now that you know that you and your small business are a likely target for a cybercrime and just how much one data breach can cost your company, let's take a closer look at exactly how these cybercriminals can attack your network and destroy your business.

CHAPTER 5

How Cybercriminals Attack Your Network

Key Takeaway: This chapter outlines exactly how your network is attacked when it is not cybersecure.

You've just learned how much damage these cybercriminals can do to your finances, customer base, reputation and ultimately your business. But how do they break into your network and cause these massive financial and productivity nightmares? There are literally dozens of ways cybercriminals can hack into your system. The following are several of today's most used methods to wreak havoc on your entire network.

Spamming

Many people think that spam is an acronym. It's not. The name came from an old Monty Python episode in which the word "spam" is repeated over and over. In the sketch, by repeating the word at increasing volume, it became both annoying and irrelevant. The nickname "spam" stuck because it perfectly describes the flood of useless, irrelevant and uninvited emails that people receive in their email inboxes.

Today, spam is still the #1 entry point into a network simply because people click links that they shouldn't. Spam also becomes a challenge when the sheer volume of unwanted emails crowds out your important business and personal messages.

Just a few years ago, spam was easy to detect because of the broken English and funky links. Today's scammers are smarter, use company logos and spell-check everything so as not to be detected. Accidentally opening and clicking on a spam link could invite threatening malware into your computers and network. Rather than wait for unwanted spam to negatively affect your business, create a proactive plan to address it. This could include software that detects and removes spam or creating anti-spam filters or rules to keep it out of your in-box.

Phishing

While most everyone can spot a spam email at a glance, phishing is much more difficult to discern. The reason is because phishing uses realistic emails in an attempt to trick recipients into sharing passwords and other sensitive information.

Cybercriminals who rely on phishing to steal passwords, private information or even money are constantly perfecting their craft to resemble the company they are trying to mimic. One widespread example of phishing mimicked Visa and told recipients that their credit card would be temporarily disabled if they didn't go to a specific website and change their password immediately. Every step of the way, from the email to the website, looked very similar to Visa's branding.

Another phishing example includes a bank email tricking an employee into providing company banking information. By sending threatening messages to specific employees, they are more likely to oblige and act too hastily. Phishing emails may also feature attached zip files that, once opened, will spread malicious viruses throughout computers and entire systems in almost no time at all.

While many Americans are now wise to never send personal information and certainly not credit card numbers or passwords via email, phishing is still a very effective entryway into businesses' computers and IT networks. Rather than deal with the embarrassment of asking their manager or boss whether or not an email is legitimate, many employees will take action on a professional-looking email. It takes just seconds to let unwanted hackers into your business network. And once they're in, there's no telling the damage they can do.

HACK PROOF CASE STUDY

Mia, CPA Firm - Combating Sophisticated Phishing Attacks

Mia's CPA firm of 15 professionals became the target of sophisticated phishing attacks, threatening their clients' financial integrity. To combat this, we implemented Weekly Phishing Simulations and a Suspicious Email Analysis Service (SEAS), complemented by Multi-Factor Authentication, to create a multi-layered defense system. This not only protected their financial data but also strengthened the firm's reputation for vigilance and trustworthiness in financial security.

Malware

A combination of the words "malicious" and "software," malware is any piece of software or code created with the intent of damaging devices or stealing data. Malware includes all malicious software, including viruses, worms, spyware, ransomware, Trojan viruses and others.

So, why do cybercriminals spend so much time creating and distributing malware? They do so with the intention of selling it online to the highest bidder for use by other criminals. Also, some cybercriminals engage in malware as a tool for protests. Others use it to test cyber security or even as weapons of war between governments.

Malware can also be used to turn a computer into a bot (robot) designed to perform malicious attacks on other computers. Therefore, even if your firewall is set up to block attacks from countries such as China or Russia, it won't block malware attacks from your local computer.

Ransomware

Ransomware is a type of malware that is exactly what it sounds like – a software that holds your computer system and sensitive information hostage until you pay the ransom for the decryption key. Imagine coming into the office and discovering that you can no longer access your customers' files, financial information or all of your research and development records for your upcoming product launch. These cybercriminals know just how important this information is to keep your revenue stream flowing, which is why they know most businesses will pay. Ransomware is typically introduced to a system through a single employee who opens something they shouldn't. Because it is often hidden in attachments, such as an "unpaid invoice" in PDF format or a package-tracking document in Word form, ransomware often looks very innocent. However, when it's opened, the malware makes it impossible to open any other documents or applications until the ransom is paid.

Emerging trends include ransomworms, such as the infamous WannaCry and NotPetya attacks. Ransomware attacks are now a part of today's cyberthreat environment, which is getting considerably more sophisticated and costlier. In August 2019, in a coordinated ransomware attack, twenty-two Texan towns had their networks hijacked. A year earlier, Atlanta's IT infrastructure was infected by ransomware. Although the city elected not to pay, they still spent upwards of $18 million to recover.

Because health care businesses must protect their patients at all cost, nearly half of all ransomware attacks target health care companies. And because most hospitals, doctor's offices, clinics and dentists have thousands of patients, paying the hacker per patient record can result in an extraordinary amount of money. The most high-profile attacks today affect large businesses and municipal governments. Even though many target specific industries, hackers are also casting large nets, including small businesses. By infecting hundreds or thousands of businesses just like yours, even if only a small percentage of them pay, they win.

HACK PROOF TIP

Given the increasing prevalence and sophistication of ransomware attacks, it is critical to implement a robust backup strategy. Regularly back up all critical data in multiple locations, including offline storage, to protect against ransomware. Ensure that these backups are tested frequently for integrity and are easily restorable in case of data loss. Having reliable backups allows you to restore your systems quickly without succumbing to ransom demands, minimizing both downtime and financial impact

Spyware

Spyware is another type of malware that can be downloaded as easily as ransomware, through the same unassuming kinds of email attachments. However, rather than holding your information hostage for a ransom, it doesn't appear to do much of anything. Behind the scenes, it's actually doing a lot. It could be logging every keystroke in your entire company or copying emails and sending all of the gathered data to the spyware's creator. Of course, the only minor indicator that your system has been infected is that it may seem a little slower than usual.

Most spyware is used in conjunction with adware to monitor your Internet and social media habits. But it's a huge privacy and security threat. Spyware can actually be used to gather personal information for the purposes of identity theft and fraud. Because you have no control over what spyware monitors or where the information is sent, it's in your best interests to prevent all spyware in the first place and do everything you can to remove it from your computers.

Adware

Most everybody knows adware when they see it. Adware, composed of the words "advertising" and "malware," typically creates annoying pop-ups that crowd your computer screen. Now, unlike other malware, adware is not as dangerous as it is merely irritating. However, it does have the capability of undermining your security settings and tracking your activities as it slows down your computer performance.

Adware is mainly used for pinpoint marketing. While spyware watches your web-browsing habits, adware serves up ads based on what you're looking for. It's similar to your grandmother's party line, where you could listen in to your neighbors' conversations. Call the operator and ask for Pizza Hut's phone number. Then, just before you call Pizza Hut, Domino's is calling to tell you about their specials. They know you want pizza so they are getting in front of you with ads to entice you to buy from them.

Worms

Worms are unique in the world of malware because they are "stand-alone." That's because worms don't need interaction to spread to other computers. Once it gains access to a network – like clicking on an innocent-looking attachment in an e-mail – the worm quickly spreads, relying on technical vulnerabilities to infiltrate the network. That's right, an Internet worm is much like a parasite. Like a tapeworm, it duplicates itself across as many computers as possible. While worms themselves are rarely dangerous, they often create backdoors in the system that allow a hacker to launch more serious malware attacks.

Trojan Viruses

Remember the story about the Trojan Horse? In the Trojan War, the Greeks secretly constructed a huge wooden horse that hid a select force of men inside. They rolled this massive horse into Troy, and before they knew what hit them, the Greeks won the war. Because it hides within plain sight (seemingly harmless programs), this form of malware is called a Trojan.

While viruses and worms can self-replicate and infect additional files and computers on your network, a Trojan introduces dangerous malware to a computer or network. These advanced forms of malware survive because they go unnoticed. While there, they can collect information, create holes in your security or take over your computer and lock you out.

Social Engineering

As societies become more educated about how to detect malware and viruses, cybercriminals must become more sophisticated to sneak into your inbox and entice you to click. Similar to phishing, social engineering is far more personal. With social engineering, the attack can range from something as simple and direct as posing as a coworker with a seemingly legitimate e-mail and asking for a password, to developing relationships online or even in person, viewing social media pictures of where a potential victim frequently visits and targeting them outside of work.

Ransomware can be designed to exploit technical vulnerabilities and sneak into your computers and network, but the simplest form of spreading it is by someone opening up the front door. That happens when hackers can outsmart your employees, and they open an email that looks like it's from a friend or colleague. The more advanced the social engineering process, the more likely someone will unknowingly invite malware into your network and business.

Cybercriminals today have an entire arsenal of weapons to attack every computer in your company as well as your network. From simple phishing, spyware and adware software to dangerous malware, costly ransomware and Trojan viruses, it's like your business is a sitting duck just waiting for the inevitable to happen. Thankfully, over the next few chapters, we will give you the strategies, tools and resources to build a formidable wall and defend yourself from these hackers and cybercriminals.

Part Two - How to HACK PROOF Your Business

In Part One we identified and exposed the many threats small business owners' face.

Now it is time to outline the necessary steps you need to take to protect your network and your business and keep your systems safe and secure. In the following chapters you will learn the most important ways and means to protect your business.

CHAPTER 6

What You Can Do NOW to Protect Your Network and Business

Key Takeaway: This chapter will walk you step by step through a comprehensive checklist of what you need to do.

After reviewing just how much you and your business stand to lose due to threats by hackers and cybercriminals, and all of the complex and subversive ways into your network, you may wonder if you even have a chance. Absolutely!

In our experience, the most proactive business owners are the ones who avoid being hacked. The more defenses you build now between your network and cybercriminals, the more likely it is you'll avoid becoming the next small-business statistic.

Taking Responsibility as a Business Owner

As a business owner myself, I understand the massive responsibilities we must assume. You're responsible for increasing revenue and growing the business. That means attracting and closing sales or bringing in new clients or patients. You're responsible for meeting payroll for your employees and ensuring they work for a quality company that provides adequate health care, training and excellent facilities. You're responsible for ensuring operations, marketing, accounting and possibly the warehouse all run smoothly.

Yet I'm shocked at the number of business owners I've met over the years who believe that managing their computers and IT infrastructure – possibly the most important aspect of their business – should be someone else's duty. Of course, nobody expects you to be the one who monitors your network, scans for viruses and installs software to optimize your system. However, as the owner or manager of your business, at the very least, you should know just how secure your network is … or isn't.

I am willing to wager that your computer network and the critical data it holds are not nearly as secure as you think they are. Because after auditing most business networks, I am usually appalled by the incompetence and irresponsibility I discover. In 98% of the computer networks we review, I find faulty or nonexistent backups, security loopholes, shoddy reporting and flawed systems that simply cost more to maintain and don't align with the operations of the business.

If you are exposed and your network gets hacked, news travels fast on social media. Your clients and your community won't be quick to forgive. A response of "Sorry, we got hacked because we didn't think it would happen to us" or "We simply didn't want to spend the money to prevent a cyberattack" will not be sufficient. They will demand answers.

Make no mistake, as a business owner, protecting your IT network and all of the private data and financial information on it is a top priority. And whether you have a computer guy, an in- house IT team or a third-party consultant who oversees all things IT in your business, who do you think your clients, partners and employees will blame if a hacker breaks in? Ultimately, they will blame you. It's your business. It's your responsibility.

HACK PROOF CASE STUDY

Emma, Non-Profit - Protecting Donor Data
Emma's non-profit, fueled by a 12-person team passionate about environmental conservation, faced a breach that compromised donor trust. We fortified their digital defenses with a Password Manager and Multi-Factor Authentication, adding an extra layer of security for accessing sensitive information, and initiated Continuous Dark Web Monitoring to detect any leaked information swiftly. This comprehensive approach restored confidence among their donors, empowering Emma and her team to focus on their mission with renewed vigor and the assurance that their supporters' information was secure.

Keep Spyware, Malware and Viruses Off Your Network

Now that you know more about all of the dangers of spyware, malware and viruses, can you see why protecting your network is even more important?Once this malicious software gets onto your business computers, it's only a matter of time before it invades your IT network and starts wreaking havoc. Often, it goes unnoticed until long after the damage is done.

You need to be extra vigilant about keeping this malware off your network. Action taken by a user is the cause of almost every successful cyberattack, whether it is malware, spyware or viruses. Cybercriminals are incredibly clever and have figured out ways to access your computer network through some of the most innocent and common daily activities.

For example, many of the clients we see infected with spyware simply downloaded a screen saver, an "enhanced" Web browser, a music file or some other enticing but unnecessary program. By simply taking this unintentional action, they unknowingly downloaded a number of spyware and malware programs.

As a result of their actions, they could no longer use their computer because of its slowness, instability and abundance of pop-ups. Sure, your computer consultant can usually clean up the mess caused by these programs, but it is still your responsibility to become educated about what you and your employees can and cannot download. The following is a short list of program types that nobody in your office should download:

- Screensavers
- Enhanced web browsers like Cool Search
- Emoticons
- Games
- Peer-to-peer file-sharing software (e.g., KaZaa,

BitTorrent)

- Music files
- "For fun" surveys
- Banners that challenge you to "punch the monkey," shoot something or answer a trivia question to win a prize
- Sweepstakes or drawings
- Any software that requires you to accept certain conditions. By agreeing to those conditions, usually outlined in small print, you are agreeing to accept third-party software

While each of those program-type files should raise a red flag and immediately be deleted, there are a wide variety of files that may or may not be harmful to your computers and network. That's where it becomes tricky. You certainly don't want to slow down productivity in your office; however, if you let just one piece of malware sneak in, it could bring your entire business to a grinding halt.

As the owner of your business, you should keep a lookout for and keep your guard up for the following types of files delivered by email. While most of these files should be harmless, all it takes is one that's packed with a dangerous payload to infiltrate your network and disrupt your entire business.

HACK PROOF TIP

To protect your network and maintain productivity, ask your IT consultant about implementing continuous monitoring of file behavior within your systems. This involves using security tools that not only scan files at the point of entry but also keep track of how files behave once inside your network. Such tools can quickly identify and isolate files that begin to act suspiciously—like attempting to encrypt data or modify system settings—thus preventing malware from executing its payload.

Executable Files

This is where all of this mayhem started. If there are any files to avoid like the plague, it's executable files. There are a couple of different types:

- .exe Files – The extension .exe marks an executable file that can become active on your computer the second you open it. Over the years, these types of executable files have carried very dangerous payloads that have infected entire networks. These files should NEVER be opened if attached to an email. Thankfully, there are many other less dangerous file formats available today. Plus, most email providers, such as Gmail and Outlook, completely block e-mails containing .exe extensions, so you'll hopefully never see them.

- HTML Files – Not too long ago, you would receive multiple HTML emails every day. Since it is the standard language used to create web pages, it was very common. However, in the .html format,Trojans and worms can easily hide. To fight the risk of accidentally releasing malware onto your system, many companies no longer allow HTML emails to hit their servers.

Text Files, PDFs and Document Files

Any business office is going to constantly send and receive text files, PDFs and document files in order to get work done. The large majority of these are legitimate files; however, all it takes is one that looks like an innocent file before it starts eating away at your network.

- .txt Files – These are generally harmless since they represent a standard text document that is recognized by Word or any word-processing program. They can also be opened using Microsoft Notepad and Apple TextEdit. However, in the year 2000, the ILOVEYOU computer worm spread rapidly across the globe. People opened it because it had a
- .txt.vbs extension, but most e-mail programs didn't

display the ".vbs" part. People opened it because they thought it was a simple text document. Instead, it did $10 billion worth of damage.

- .pdf Files – Everyone knows PDF files. Most of the time, they are harmless files opened with Adobe Reader. However, there are many security gaps that allow cybercriminals to transport malware onto your computer using PDF files. If you don't recognize who is sending the PDF, think twice before opening it and downloading it. Beware of links within PDF documents that take you to a remote website or download a malicious payload.
- .doc / .docx / .xls / .xlsx / .ppt / .pptx Files – These are all Office documents that are commonly e-mailed. The danger in opening these files is that they could contain macro viruses. Starting with Office 2007, Microsoft made a helpful change by alerting you of a file containing potential harmful macros with the extension .docm. However, a .doc file may or may not contain macros. Beware of links within these documents, especially if they take you to a remote site or download dangerous malware.

Certainly you can't adopt a policy to never accept emails with .pdf files or .doc files. That could be a nightmare for your team's productivity. However, you can be proactive in how you handle these files. First, confirm with the sender that they intentionally sent the file you received. If you weren't expecting an e-mail with a file attachment, simply double-check with them. Second, if you receive an email with a .doc attachment, ask the sender if they could resend the file as a .pdf, which could be less of a risk.

Image Files

The extension .jpg represents an image or picture file. If you run an advertising agency, photography studio or architectural firm, you would naturally receive these types of files on a daily basis. However, most businesses have little reason to receive .jpg files, especially when they can easily be turned into less risky

.pdf files.

The reason .jpg files could be harmful to your network is that the extension is often used to camouflage an executable program. Make sure your e-mail program displays the complete file extension to lessen the risk of a malicious attachment.

Audio Files

Audio files are typically sent as a recording of a webinar, videoconferencing call or presentation. Therefore, they should not be a regular occurrence in most companies. If your employees tend to send and receive many audio files, you may inquire if they are exchanging songs via your company email. You certainly don't want to put your entire business at risk because employees are violating company email policies.

- .mp3 Files – These audio files are generally safe. But always double-check with the sender prior to opening.
- .wav Files – Audio data in a WAV file is not compressed. These files tend to be much larger in size than .mp3 files. Because it's not compressed, .wav can be a much easier file type to hide malware. Always be suspicious of any .wav attachments that come across your network.

Video Files

Like audio files, large video files are excellent hiding places for malware. You'll know it's a video file by the extension: .mpg/ .mpeg / .avi / .wmv / .mov / .ram. Again, most businesses don't exchange video files on a regular basis. If one of your employees gets bombarded by multiple emails with video file attachments on a daily basis, inquire if it's truly necessary or unrelated to business.

Compressed Files

Compressed files, like .zip and .rar files, pose a significant risk for businesses like yours. That's because they can contain viruses that become active as soon as you extract them. Always make sure you trust the origin of the e-mail attachment before opening.

Beware of Additional Entry Points

If hackers really want to break into your network, they have more options than hoping your employees click on their email attachment. If you don't have the most up-to-date security patches and virus definitions installed, wrongdoers can access your computer in other ways. Most spyware and virus attacks are the result of an end user (such as an employee, business owner or partner) downloading a questionable file or program, disabling their antivirus software or somehow circumventing security settings or acceptable-use policies set by your computer guy or IT consultant.

Many businesses have hardware or software inadequacies that may not be able to be controlled or prevented by typical computer consultants. Also, many business owners don't want to pay for their consultants to perform simple preventive maintenance, update security patches and virus definitions or monitor their system's performance. This lack of maintenance is an invitation for problems that could become massive inconveniences that affect your time and wallet.

A Good Firewall Is Essential

Don't scrimp on a good firewall. A firewall acts as the frontline defense against hackers blocking everything you haven't specifically allowed to enter (or leave) your computer network. As with all devices on your network, firewalls need monitoring and maintenance. Your company IT person or consultant should include your firewall as part of their regular maintenance of your network.

There are several reasons why your business will benefit from a strong firewall:

- Block access to unapproved websites. You can set up a firewall to block access to social media sites, betting sites, sports sites and other time wasters.
- Protect your business from malicious code. Strong firewalls can inspect the traffic going into and out of your network. All day, every day, your firewall can detect and block viruses, worms, spam and other unwanted Internet traffic. Plus, they will log intrusion attempts as well as block malicious applications while allowing access to the good ones.
- Better control your bandwidth. Beyond providing security, you can actually meter and limit your network bandwidth. By curtailing non-business traffic, such as videos, music and images, you'll have more bandwidth for essential business

applications.

- Provide VPN services. Today, firewalls can provide site-to- site connectivity through virtual private networks (VPNs), which allow users at remote sites to securely access your internal network resources. Now, any work-from-home employees, as well as traveling employees and contractors, can increase their productivity and collaboration by securely accessing your network.

Train Your Employees

Because we're talking about safeguarding your computers, network and data, we tend to think that the best defense should also be electronic. While installing virus and malware detection software is critical to keeping your important data out of the wrong hands, your first line of defense should be the people in and around your office. Yes, you and your employees. Training your employees on how to properly use your technology and how to identify potential cyberthreats is essential to staying one step ahead of the cybercriminals.

HACK PROOF CASE STUDY

Karen, HR company - Securing Confidential Employee Data

Karen's HR company, a trusted entity of 20 employees dedicated to career development, was rattled by the threat of insider data breaches. We introduced Complete Endpoint Threat Detection & Response to keep a vigilant eye on sensitive information and launched Quarterly Security Awareness Training to embed a culture of cybersecurity awareness. This transformed Karen's company into a secure haven for personal data, where trust in protecting employee information was restored and reinforced.

Tucking this vital information into the back of an employee manual is simply not sufficient. Neither is a one time staff training that will be ignored and forgotten. You and your entire team should have a basic understanding of the methods of cybercrime, as well as regular updates on computer security protocol and the latest in cybercrime tactics and defenses. Your employees should have an in-depth understanding and proactive resolve to ensure the best practices toward passwords, keeping a clean space, identifying malicious emails, proper communication, social engineering and encrypting emails. More information about encrypting emails is covered later in this chapter.

Create and Enforce an Acceptable Use Policy (AUP)

Training your employees goes beyond teaching them about being diligent in spotting a malicious email. Everyone on your team needs to be aware of how they can actively protect your business from cybercrime. You can accomplish this by circulating Internet security policies, also known as acceptable use policies (AUP) or fair use policies. These are written documents created by the business owner that clearly state precisely what employees, subcontractors and end users can and can't do in regard to accessing the Internet, company computers and e-mail while working for your business.

You should require everyone who accesses your network in any capacity to sign the acceptable use policy before they are able to access your Internet, computers or e-mail. By requiring an agreement, AUPs ensure your end users are explicitly aware of their rights and responsibilities.

HACK PROOF TIP

Make security awareness a core part of your company culture by conducting impromptu quizzes, sending fake phishing emails to educate employees, and rewarding those who report vulnerabilities. Remember, a well-trained employee is your best defense against cyber attacks!

For example, employees should not be allowed to download or access programs, screensavers, pictures, music files or file- sharing networks. Not only will this save precious bandwidth, it also prevents accidentally downloading viruses and spyware. An AUP should also educate employees on the appropriate use of your company's resources.

If you don't want your staff to download pornographic material and send racist jokes through a company email account, for instance, you have to communicate this information to them in an AUP and have them acknowledge in writing that they have read and understood it. Your IT consultant can help you draft this document and enforce the policies outlined in it.

There are multiple reasons why you should consider an AUP for your business:

- First, it ensures the safety of the users. By clearly outlining prohibitions and rights, it can help deter illegal or offensive behavior that can damage the reputation of the organization or endanger users. Examples of this include the sale of counterfeit goods or outlining standard practice for commenting on blog posts.
- Second, AUPs can protect the business from any legal action. In case of any legal action or cybercrimes associated with your company's website, the acceptable use policy proves the company has taken reasonable measures to protect the interests of users.
- Third, they can safeguard the organization's reputation. Any business, especially those that engage with customers online, should make an effort to show due diligence in regard to cyber security and safety.
- Fourth, AUPs enhance ease of use and productivity. Business owners and managers don't want to pay for employees who waste company time on Facebook, YouTube and other non-productive sites. An AUP guides end users and customers on acceptable practices.
- Fifth, AUPs better regulate employees using their own personal devices. If an employee is checking unregulated, personal email on their own laptop

and their laptop gets infected by malware, a hacker now has a gateway to enter YOUR network. Also, what happens if that employee leaves the company?

Create and Enforce a Bring Your Own Device (BYOD) Policy

A BYOD policy allows employees to bring in personal mobile devices and use these devices to access company data, e-mail, etc. While inviting in computers and devices from home may be convenient and a way to curb costs, it also invites new opportunities to breach your network and access your company data.

Questions you should ask:

Are you permitted to erase company data from their personal laptop or phone? If not, what happens if those devices get into the wrong hands and hackers suddenly have direct access to your servers? You must protect your business with an AUP that permits you to remotely wipe any device so your company data isn't compromised.

Further, if the data in your organization is highly sensitive, such as patient records, credit card information, financial information and the like, you may not be legally permitted to allow employees to access it on personal devices that are not secured. Of course, this doesn't usually happen in a malicious way. An employee may innocently take work home with them. If it's a company-owned device, you need to detail what an employee can or cannot do with that device, including "rooting" or "jailbreaking" the device to circumvent security mechanisms you put in place.

Creating Better Passwords

Of course, it's much easier to remember the same password you've used a million times before ... or one featuring your birthdate or your daughter's name ... or simply using "password" (which, even after countless jokes and warnings, is still one of today's most frequently used passwords). And yes, it can be a pain to have to reset your password each time you forget it. But, for the security of your company's network and data, it's well worth the extra time and inconvenience to create very secure passwords.

Generally, the longer the password, the more secure. Ideally, it should include at least one special character, one number and both uppercase and lowercase letters. But once you land on that perfect password, don't use it for multiple applications. Create new passwords for each new application used. Also, two-factor authentication should be in place every time a password is required. Two-factor authentication is an extra layer of protection that ensures only the person who is supposed to access the account can access it. Simply knowing the password would not be sufficient.

Also, it should go without saying that your password should be kept to yourself and not shared with anyone else, including coworkers, partners, friends and family. In addition, if you must terminate an employee, or upon them resigning, make sure their passwords are no longer active.

Many of your employees probably utilize auto-fill passwords. After all, in less than a second, your password is automatically filled in and you're zipping through the Internet without having to remember your password or request a password reset. There are also password-manager applications that make it a cinch to log in. Problem is, hackers know these are a gold mine to all of your private data.

Rather than keeping your passwords on a spreadsheet or a notepad that could easily be compromised, it's better to utilize a password manager. Therefore, you only need to remember one master password and the password manager houses all of your passwords. While a password manager could potentially be hacked, it's far safer than keeping a password file on your computer.

HACK PROOF TIP

To protect your browsers from password theft, we recommend turning off this auto-fill option. Please note that depending on the browser you are using (Chrome, Firefox or Safari), the directions to turn off password auto-fill will vary.

Keep a Clean Work Space

"How you do anything is how you do everything." – T. Harv Eker, author, businessman and motivational speaker. If your employees have a messy workspace, odds are their computer desktops are also disheveled and unorganized. I bet their cars and homes are equally as cluttered. On the flipside, when you can see the entire desktop, you can bet that person also has a clean computer desktop with files neatly organized.

Both your employees' computer desktops and actual desks should be kept clean, with no material on them that isn't relevant to work function. Also, leaving passwords or other personal material on, in or around one's desk is also a recipe for potential disaster.

Know How to Identify Malicious Emails

Your entire team must be vigilant to spot, question and delete potential threats delivered via email. When your employees begin from the stance that EVERY email contains possible malware, you have many more defenders who will help protect your computers and network.

It only takes a second to evaluate an incoming e-mail and determine if it's a potential threat. Look for clues that could send up red flags, including:

- Unfamiliar domain names as part of the sender's e-mail address

- Short, vague and irrelevant messages with links attached
- Unexpected links with no explanation
- Innocuous attachments to vague and / or unfamiliar e-mails
- Incorrect spelling or bad grammar
- Asking for personal information
- A threatening or panic-causing message

One recent type of email attack is called a man-in-the-middle attack, where the hacker secretly intercepts communications between two parties. These types of attacks can be identified because when you click on a link in the email, nothing happens. But something IS happening: the hacker may gain remote access to your computer. If you ever click a link and think nothing happened, play it safe and report it to your IT consultant.

Give each employee a tip sheet to keep on their desk regarding these types of suspicious emails. In addition, encourage your employees to call the sender if they are ever in doubt. Simply e-mailing the sender to inquire if it's legitimate may not be enough if their email has been compromised. As these phishing emails and attempts to break into companies' systems continue to evolve, regular briefings of all employees should be an important part of your business structure.

Keep Communication Open

You've heard the saying "See something, say something." Well, that applies to cyber security as well. If an email, web page or attachment looks or seems suspicious, assume it is. Of course, you should avoid clicking the link or opening the attachment. Beyond that, you should also alert your IT consultant. If your consultant does recognize it as a potential cyberattack, make sure everyone on the team knows what the attempted attack looks like so they can identify possible future attacks.

Fact is, most cybercriminals are trying to infiltrate an entire business, not simply stop at one person. So, if anyone in your organization spots a potential attack, odds are their colleagues could be hit next. If they are working through your whole team, a heads-up will likely prevent any slips in security.

If anyone on your team is unable to recognize and avert a cyberattack, encourage them not to hide it because of embarrassment. Instead, own it. Let everyone know what the attack looks like, how to either delete it or avoid it and the ways in which it affected your business. Once your employees clearly understand that this is far more dangerous than just nuisance spam, you'll have everyone looking out for it.

Destroy Old Data

People have a tendency to simply "throw away" computers and hardware when they get new technologies. This is a mistake. Obsolete computers should not only be wiped clean before being trashed or donated, their hard drives should be completely destroyed. This proactive measure should also be done to printers or any devices that store data for any length of time.

Just think of everything that's on your computer: passwords, customer files, private and financial data. You may think it's trash, but a cybercriminal sees it as treasure. And rather than having to hack your network, he simply plucks your old computer from the trash or recycle center. Don't make it easy for them!

Protect Your WiFi Network

It seems just a few years ago, free WiFi access was a rarity. Today, most customers and clients expect free access to a guest WiFi network. While you want to better serve those in your office or place of business, you certainly don't want to offer cybercriminals one more access point into your network.

So, to keep customers happy and criminals away, here are a few rules to follow when setting up your WiFi:

- Don't give guests access to your primary WiFi. It doesn't take a veteran hacker to break into your company network using your WiFi as an access point. Almost anyone with a slight technical background could do it. And once they're in, all of your confidential data, customer information, credit cards and passwords can be stolen. Make it a point to provide a full security stack solution on all tablets and devices and even your phones. Nobody should be allowed to access the company WiFi unless it is fully protected.

- Create a separate guest WiFi. If the router in your office supports a built-in guest WiFi feature, you can create a separate "virtual" network. In other words, your guests and clients can jump online without accessing your company's primary network.
- Restrict bandwidth and distance. While you may want to offer Internet access to your customers, you shouldn't do so at the expense of your own business productivity. Therefore, since your guest WiFi still utilizes your ISP connection, you should limit total bandwidth usage on your guest network. Visitors usually engage in higher-bandwidth activities, such as streaming TV shows, watching videos and playing music. In addition to restricting bandwidth, you should ensure your router doesn't allow people outside of your office or building to access the guest WiFi, again eating up valuable bandwidth and also putting your business at more risk for cybercrime.

Encrypt Emails

By now, you realize that emails are one of the most frequently used entry points for delivering malware. Aside from that significant threat, even amateur hackers can easily intercept and steal just about any information you send via email. Thankfully, the large majority of the e-mails people tend to send do not contain financial information or private content you don't want to get into the wrong hands.

However, on occasion, you or your employee may need to send information that would expose your business if a hacker stole it. Rather than waiting to send via certified mail or another slow method, you can now easily encrypt your email to add another layer of protection. While the most sophisticated cybercriminals may still be able to decrypt it and access your private communications, encrypting is one of today's most secure ways to protect your emails.

So, how does email encryption work? You have both a public key and a private key, which is known as public key infrastructure. While your public key is handed out to anyone you choose, such as your entire office, your family and your friends, or even made public, your private key is known only by you.

When someone on your team wants to send you a message that is meant only for you to see, they would encrypt it using your public key. However, your private key is required to decrypt the message. If, at that point, someone intercepted your email, it would look like useless gibberish. Aside from encrypting your message, you can also use your private key to digitally sign the message so the recipient is confident it came from you.

HACK PROOF TIP

The best advice is to never send account information, passwords or credit card information via email. However, if there is no other viable method of transferring that private information, make sure you are using encryption software.

Be Aware of Sneaky Ways Hackers Invade Your Network

While your entire team should be aware of the most common ways cybercriminals can attack your network, they should also know about the lesser-used sneaky ways they can invade. After all, if they're only focused on the most basic ways your system can be compromised, you are not mitigating all of the risks.

Not too long ago, Microsoft released a security bulletin about three newly discovered vulnerabilities that could allow an attacker to gain control of your computer. How? Simply by tricking you into downloading and opening a maliciously crafted picture.

Along with the warning, Microsoft released a Windows update to correct these vulnerabilities. Problem was, if you didn't have a process to ensure you were applying critical updates as soon as they became available, you were still completely vulnerable to this attack.

HACK PROOF CASE STUDY

John, Wealth Management - Ensuring Financial Fortitude

John's wealth management firm, where 30 professionals manage clients' life savings, was at risk from cyber espionage. We wrapped their communications and transactions in End-to-End Encryption and implemented Cloud Layer Detection and Response, along with Continuous Dark Web Monitoring, securing their clients' financial futures against any form of digital intrusion, reinforcing John's role as a trusted guardian of wealth

Want another compelling reason to ensure your network stays up-to-date on the latest security patches? Most hackers don't discover these security loopholes on their own. Rather, they learn about them when Microsoft or any other software vendor announces the vulnerability and issues an update. That is the hackers' cue to spring into action. They immediately analyze the update and craft a way to exploit it using malware or a virus. In no time, they have a way to infiltrate any computer or network that has not yet installed the security patch. And the time between the release of the update and the release of the exploit that targets the vulnerability is getting shorter every day.

When the "Nimda" worm was first discovered in 2001, for instance, Microsoft had released the patch that protected against that vulnerability 331 days before. Network administrators had plenty of time to apply the update, yet because so many failed to do so, the Nimda ("admin" spelled backwards) worm caused lots of damage.

Clearly, your IT consultant needs to be paying close attention to your systems to ensure that critical updates are applied as soon as they are announced. That's why we highly recommend that small-business owners without a full-time IT staff allow their consultant to monitor and maintain their network.

Have an Excellent Backup

Ransomware is one of today's most popular and aggressive cybercrime attacks, where a hacker locks up your files and holds them for ransom until you pay a fee to access them. The second you get that notice on your computer screen that you can no longer access your files is the very second you regret not having a backup system in place. Because if your files are backed up, you don't have to pay a crook to get them back.

A good backup will also protect you against an employee accidentally (or intentionally) deleting or overwriting files. Natural disasters, fire, water damage, hardware failures and a host of other data-erasing disasters can all be made less horrific if you have a quality backup system in place. While your hardware may be a total loss in some disasters, your important data and private customer information will still be whole and accessible.

Your backups should be automated and monitored. Ensure your IT consultant has a policy in place to test every month. In addition, they should get notifications of data usage so they can monitor fluctuations and oddities. The worst time to test your backup system is when you desperately need it to work!

Check Before You Connect

We live in a world today where speed is essential and portability is expected. It seems everyone has multiple flash drives or thumb drives to plug into a computer's USB port to quickly save and exchange data, images, videos, etc. Problem is, because they are so prevalent, we don't always remember who we got these portable drives from and what information is contained on the drive. There are countless examples of using an innocent USB drive or CD to upload malware onto a computer or network. Unless you know exactly what's on the device and you trust the person who gave you the device, don't let it onto your system!

Now you have multiple ways to defend your network and protect your data, financial information and ultimately your business. Again, being proactive is key. I also strongly advise implementing as many of these security measures as you can. Simply having a strong firewall and capable backup system may not be enough.

One security measure many business owners are flocking to is the cloud. Along with ease, convenience and cost savings, the cloud offers your business an added layer of security. This next chapter takes us into the cloud.

HACK PROOF TIP

Introduce a "Safe Device" protocol where all external storage devices like USBs or CDs are checked and scanned in a quarantined computer system before use on the network. This system should not have access to your main network and is specifically used to test external devices for malware or suspicious content. By doing so, you significantly lower the risk of inadvertently introducing malware into your network. This practice not only protects your data but also educates your employees about the potential dangers of unchecked devices.

CHAPTER 7

Better Security in the Cloud

Key Takeaway: This chapter defines cloud computing, the pro's and con's and what you will need to do if you want a cloud based platform for your business.

While cloud computing has technically been around since the 1960s, the "cloud" as we know it first appeared in 2011 with IBM's SmartCloud and Apple's ICloud. Yet, so many people today are still confused about exactly what the cloud is and how it can enhance their business. In this chapter, we will answer all of your questions about the cloud and how it may even bolster your network security.

What Exactly Is Cloud Computing?

Wikipedia defines cloud computing as "the use and access of multiple server-based computational resources via a digital network (WAN, Internet connection using the World Wide Web, etc.)."

But as a business owner or manager, you simply want to know how the cloud can enhance your productivity and even improve your cyber security. So, to help you better understand how cloud computing can positively impact your business and computer network, let's compare it to the evolution of public utilities and electricity.

Back in the industrial age, in order for factories to produce their sellable goods they had to also produce their own electricity. Whether in the manufacture of textiles or railroad spikes, using machines gave these companies enormous competitive advantages by producing more goods with fewer workers and in less time. For years, the businesses that flourished were those that were capable of producing their own power. As a result, the production of power was every bit as important as the skill of their workers and quality of their products.

Therefore, factories had to master two crafts: producing their goods and producing power. Fortunately, Thomas Edison found a solution to this widespread problem. He developed a commercial-grade replacement for gas lighting and heating that was centrally sourced. Suddenly, electricity could be distributed to the many factories that needed it.

The concept of electric current being generated in central power plants and then delivered to factories caught on fast. At that point, electricity became a utility. No longer did manufacturers have to be in the business of producing their own power with expensive waterwheels. In no time, factories that took advantage of this new lower-cost option offered by public utilities were at a competitive advantage. Almost overnight, thousands of steam engines and electric generators were rendered obsolete in those factories.

While Edison's invention and ingenuity made this possible, what really drove the demand was pure economics. Utility companies were able to leverage economies of scale that single manufacturing plants simply couldn't match in output or in price. Beyond flowing into every factory, the price of power dropped so significantly that it was suddenly being used in just about every household in America.

Today, technological advancements are providing us similar advantages. The only difference is that instead of cheap and plentiful electricity, advancements in technology and Internet connectivity are driving down the costs of computing power. Just like paying for a utility, with cloud computing, businesses can pay for "computing power" without having to absorb the exorbitant costs of installing, hosting and supporting the technology on-premise.

Did you know, you are probably already experiencing the benefits of cloud computing in some capacity? Below are a number of cloud computing applications or "software as a service" (SaaS) you might be using right now:

- Gmail, Hotmail or other free email accounts
- Facebook, X (previously Twitter), LinkedIn, Instagram and other social media
- ZohoCRM, Hubspot, NetSuite, Salesforce and other customer relationship management software
- Constant Contact, KEAP, AWeber or other email broadcasting services
- Typeform, SurveyMonkey and other online survey tools
- All things Google (search, ads, maps, etc.)

Fact is, almost every application you use today can be (or already is) put "in the cloud," where you can access it and pay for it via your browser for a monthly fee just like utility pricing. You don't purchase and install software but instead access it via an Internet browser.

Microsoft 365 and Google Workspace are perfect examples of how people today want and need cloud computing. For a reasonable monthly or annual fee, you get full access and use of Office applications that used to cost a few hundred dollars to purchase. And, since these apps are being powered by the cloud provider, you don't need an expensive computer with lots of power to use them – just a simple Internet connection is all you need on a laptop, desktop or tablet.

HACK PROOF TIP

As your business utilizes more cloud-based services, it's crucial to conduct regular audits of who has access to what within these platforms. Set a schedule to review and update access permissions every quarter. This ensures that only the right people have the right level of access, especially as roles change over time. Removing access for former employees or downgrading access when someone changes positions are important steps in safeguarding your sensitive data and preventing data leaks or breaches within cloud environments.

Pros and Cons of Moving to the Cloud

Please keep in mind there is no "perfect" solution. All of your options have upsides and downsides that need to be evaluated on a case-by-case basis. Many "cloud experts" out there will convince you that cloud computing is the only way to go. Sure, it's their expertise, but it's also how they get paid. Expecting otherwise would be like going to a Toyota dealership and waiting for the salesperson to give you an honest opinion about Nissans and Hondas. Their goal is to sell you a Toyota.

It's possible that the best option for you is a hybrid solution where some of your applications and functionality are in the cloud and some are still hosted and maintained from an in-house server. Here are the general pros and cons of cloud computing:

Pros of Cloud Computing

- Lowered IT costs. This is probably the single most compelling reason why companies choose to move their network to the cloud. Not only do you save money on software licenses, but you also save on hardware (servers and workstations) as well as on IT support and upgrades. Rather than constantly writing cash-flow-draining checks for IT upgrades because the technology is constantly improving, you may save quite a bit by considering cloud computing.
- Freedom and convenience. One of the major reasons people prefer cloud computing is the ability to access your desktop and/or applications from anywhere and any device. If you travel a lot, have remote workers or prefer to use an iPad while traveling and a laptop at your house, cloud computing will give you the ability to work from any of these devices at any location. Gone are the days when employees were confined to a desk. Considering there are over 3.5 billion smartphones in use today, cloud computing ensures everyone is kept in the loop. Through the cloud, you can

offer conveniently accessible information to sales staff who travel, freelance employees or remote employees.

- Flexibility. The cloud offers businesses like yours more flexibility versus hosting on a local server. Need extra bandwidth? Cloud computing can meet that demand instantly without the massive time and expense of upgrading your IT infrastructure. With a cloud-focused approach to your business, you have far more freedom and flexibility to positively impact your overall efficiency.
- Use it without "owning" it. You don't own the responsibility of having to install, update and maintain your IT infrastructure. It's like living in a condo where someone else takes care of the building and landscape maintenance. They handle all plumbing issues and keep up the lawn, but you still have access to all facilities. This "use it without owning it" approach is particularly attractive for companies that are new or expanding, and don't want the heavy outlay of cash for purchasing and supporting an expensive computer network.
- "Greener" technology. Yes, switching to cloud-based applications can actually save on power and your electric bill. Of course, smaller businesses may not see much if any savings. However, for larger companies that need to constantly cool a server closet with multiple servers that must run

24/7/365, the savings can be considerable.

- More robust security. There's a common fear that security can be an issue when you adopt a cloud-computing solution. That's because people think it's more difficult to protect something that's not physically in their office. When important data is kept securely onsite, you believe that data is better protected. If you're not exactly sure where your files are in the cloud, how can you be sure cybercriminals aren't accessing them remotely? That's the concern, at least

  Security in a cloud-computing environment is very robust. First, a cloud host's primary job is to carefully monitor security. In a conventional in-house environment, your IT team must divide their time between many IT concerns, including security. Second, one of the biggest sources of cyberattacks includes internal data theft perpetrated by employees. With the threat of internal data theft, it can actually be much safer to keep sensitive information off-site.

  According to RapidScale, 94% of businesses noticed an improvement in IT security after they switched to the cloud. That's because the data is being encrypted and is transmitted over networks and stored in databases. This advanced encryption makes it even more difficult for hackers to access and steal your data. Also, the data centers must follow strict compliance and regulations while being tested each year. In most cases, there are security cameras, keypads and fingerprint scanners just to enter the lobby area of these data centers. Beyond the lobby, devices are protected in cabinets behind locked cages.

- Disaster recovery is instantaneous. The server in your office is extremely vulnerable to multiple threats. Viruses, human error, hardware failure, software corruption, and even physical damage due to a fire, flooding or other natural disaster are all very possible. If your server was in the cloud and your office was flooded, you could simply purchase a new laptop and be back up and running that same day. Of course, if you had a traditional network with tape drives, CDs, USB drives or other physical storage devices to back up your system, it could take weeks to get back up and running. Even then, you may have lost all of your data, including financial information, customers' accounts and private information, as well as all of your employees' work!
- Loss prevention. If you are not investing in a cloud-computing solution, all of your valuable data is tied directly to the office computers it resides in. For now, that may not be an issue. However, computers and servers will crash at some point. And when that

happens, you just might end up permanently losing all of your critical data. This is far more common than you might imagine, since computers can malfunction for many reasons, from viral infections to hardware deterioration to simple user error. Did you know that 10,000 laptops are reported lost or stolen every week at major airports? If you aren't in the cloud, you risk losing all of the important data and projects that have built your business to what it is today.

- Plus, like a public utility, cloud platforms are far more robust and secure than your average business network because they can utilize economies of scale to invest heavily into security, redundancy and failover systems, making them far less likely to go down.
- Automatic software updates. Cloud-based applications automatically refresh and update themselves, instead of forcing an IT department to perform a manual organization-wide update. Not only can you save critical time with automated software updates, you can save money by not spending more on internal or external IT resources.

Cons of Cloud Computing

- The Internet goes offline. While you can mitigate this risk by using a commercial-grade Internet connection and maintaining a second backup connection, there is still a chance you'll lose Internet connectivity, making it impossible to work.

- Data security. You've just learned that data in the cloud can be safer than simply storing it on computers and / or a server that resides in your office; however, many people still feel uncomfortable about having their data stored "invisibly" in an off-site location. So, before you choose any cloud provider, you need to find out more information about where they are storing your data, how it is encrypted, who has access and how you can get it back.
- Compliance issues. There are a number of laws and regulations, such as Gramm-Leach-Bliley, Sarbanes-Oxley and HIPAA, that require companies to control and protect their data. They also require businesses to certify that they have knowledge and control over who can access the data, who sees it and how and where it is stored. In a public cloud environment, this can be an issue since many cloud providers won't tell you specifically where your data is stored.
- Most cloud providers have SAS 70 certifications, which require them to be able to describe exactly what is happening in their environment, how and where the data comes in, what the provider does with it and what controls are in place over the access to and processing of the data. However, as

the business owner, it's your neck on the line if the data is compromised, so it's important that you ask for some type of validation that they are meeting the various compliance regulations on an ongoing basis.

HACK PROOF TIP

When selecting a cloud provider, insist on transparency and regular compliance reporting. Require your provider to furnish detailed reports on their compliance with relevant regulations and standards, such as GDPR, HIPAA, or PCI DSS, depending on your industry. These reports should include specifics on data encryption methods, access controls, and audit logs. Additionally, ask for the ability to conduct or commission independent security audits of their services periodically.

Migration Gotchas! What You Need to Know About Transitioning to a Cloud-Based Network

When done right, a migration to Microsoft 365 or another cloud solution should be like any other migration. There's planning that needs to be done, prerequisites that have to be determined and the inevitable "quirks" that need to be ironed out once you make the move.

Every company has its own unique environment, so it's

practically impossible to try and plan for every potential pitfall; however, here are some BIG things you want to ask your IT consultant about before making the leap.

- **Downtime.** Some organizations cannot afford any downtime, while others can do without their network for a day or two. Make sure you communicate your specific needs regarding downtime, and make sure your IT provider has a solid plan to prevent extended downtime.
- **Painfully slow performance.** Ask your IT consultant if there's any way you can run your network in a test environment before making the full migration. Imagine how frustrated you would be if you migrate your network and discover everything is running so slow you can barely work! Again, every environment is slightly different, so it's best to test before you transition.
- **Third-party applications.** If your organization has plug- ins to Exchange for faxing, voice mail or integration into another application, make sure you test to see if it will still work in the new environment

Different Types of Cloud Solutions

- **Pure Cloud.** In this solution, all of your applications and data are put on the other side of the firewall (in the cloud) and accessed through various devices (laptops, desktops, iPads, phones) via the Internet.

This is the most **common type of cloud solution.**

- **Hybrid Cloud**. Although "pure" cloud computing has valid applications, for many it's downright scary. And in some cases it is NOT the smartest move, due to compliance issues, security restrictions, speed and performance. A hybrid cloud solution enables you to put certain pieces of existing IT infrastructure (storage and email) in the cloud, and the remainder of the IT infrastructure stays on-premise. This gives you the ability to enjoy the cost savings and benefits of cloud computing where it makes the most sense without risking your entire environment.
- **Single Point Solutions.** Another option would be to simply put certain applications, like SharePoint or Microsoft Exchange, in the cloud while keeping everything else on-site. Since e-mail is usually a critical application that everyone needs and wants access to on the road and on various devices (iPad, smartphone, etc.), often this is a great way to get advanced features of Microsoft Exchange without the cost of installing and supporting your own in-house Exchange server.
- **Public Cloud Vs. Private Cloud.** A public cloud is a service that anyone can tap into with a network connection and a credit card. They are shared infrastructures that allow you to pay as you go and are managed through a self-service web

portal. Private clouds are essentially self- built infrastructures that mimic public cloud services, but are on-premise. Private clouds are often the choice of companies that want the benefits of cloud computing but don't want their data held in a public environment.

Cloud Computing FAQs

Q1. Could I keep a local copy of my data in case we lose access to the cloud?

Answer: We resolve this by keeping a synchronized copy of your data on your on-site server as well as in the cloud. Here's how this works: Microsoft offers a feature with Windows called "DFS," which stands for Distributed File Systems. This technology synchronizes documents between cloud servers and local servers in your office. So, instead of getting rid of your old server, we keep it on-site and maintain an up-to-date synched copy of your files, folders and documents on it.

If the Internet goes down or slows to a grind, you simply open a generic folder on your PC and the system will automatically know to pull the documents from the fastest location. Once a file is modified, it syncs it in seconds so you don't have to worry about having multiple versions of the same document. Using this process, you get the benefits of cloud with a backup solution to keep you up and running during slow periods or complete Internet outages.

Q2. What about security? Isn't there a big risk of someone accessing my data if it's in the cloud?

Answer: In many cases, cloud computing is a MORE secure way of accessing and storing data. Just because your server is on- site doesn't make it more secure; in fact, most small to medium businesses can't justify the cost of securing their network the way a cloud provider can. And most security breaches occur due to human error – one of your employees downloads a file that contains a virus, they don't use secure passwords or they simply e-mail confidential information out to people who shouldn't see it.

Q3. What if you go out of business? How do I get my data back?

Answer: We present network documentation that clearly outlines where your data is and how you could get it back in the event of an emergency. This includes emergency contact numbers, detailed information on how to access your data and infrastructure without needing our assistance, a copy of our insurance policy and information regarding your backups and licensing.

We also give you a copy of our disaster recovery plan, which shows what we've put in place to make sure we stay up and running.

Q4. Do I have to purchase new hardware (servers, workstations) to move to the cloud?

Answer: No! That's one of the selling points of cloud computing. It allows you to use older workstations, laptops and servers, because the computing power is in the cloud. Not only does that allow you to keep and use hardware longer, but it allows you to save on workstations and laptops because you don't need the expensive computing power required in the past.

What to look for when hiring an IT consultant to move your network to the cloud.

Unfortunately, the IT consulting industry has its share of incompetent or unethical people who will try to take advantage of trusting business owners who simply do not have the ability to determine whether or not they know what they are doing. Sometimes this is out of greed for your money; more often it's simply because they don't have the skills and competency to do the job right but won't tell you that up front because they want to make the sale.

Automotive repair shops, electricians, plumbers, lawyers, realtors, dentists, doctors, accountants, etc., are heavily regulated to protect the consumer from receiving substandard work or getting ripped off. However, the computer industry is still highly unregulated, and there are few laws in existence to protect the consumer – which is why it's so important for you to really research the company or person you are considering, to make sure they have the experience to set up, migrate and support your network in the cloud.

HACK PROOF TIP

When hiring an IT consultant to move your network to the cloud, it's essential to thoroughly verify their credentials and seek references. Look for certifications relevant to cloud computing from established industry organizations like Microsoft, Amazon, or Cisco. Also, request case studies or contact information for past clients that are similar to your business in scope and size.

CHAPTER 8

Preventing Identity Theft

Key Takeaway: By defining identity theft you are better able to avoid it. How to prevent it from happening to you.

What Exactly Is Identity Theft?

Most everybody has had at least one fraudulent charge appear on their credit card statement. While it wasn't your purchase, you still had to jump through several hoops to get it removed from your account. That's considerable time, energy and frustration for something you didn't even do! Or when you go to file your taxes and realize someone else has already received YOUR refund by using your information. We all know how difficult it is to deal with the simplest of IRS issues, much less proving you didn't file already.

Now imagine having your entire identity stolen. Now you're not just facing one fraudulent charge, but EVERYTHING. Your social security number, business

ID number, access to your personal and business bank accounts, retirement accounts – all swiped out from under you. Your personal and business credit cards can be maxed out too. And if they have your debit card information, your checking account could fall to zero in no time. What's even worse, you could lose your client database, financial records and all of the work files your company has ever produced or compiled. That's identity theft.

Think back to all of the time you invested to get one or two fraudulent charges taken care of. Now imagine what would happen if you had to invest an enormous amount of time, money and energy to try to restore your credit and good reputation. Think about how much your business would suffer if one day your payroll money or the money you use to pay vendors was stolen.

Even worse, what if a cybercriminal stole your identity for the purpose of pulling off other criminal acts? Yes, that happens. Could your business survive a front-page news story about how you or your company ripped off hundreds of people? Think you're "innocent until proven guilty"? Not when it comes to the eyes of the media, your customers and your competitors!

But That Could Never Happen to Me!

No business owner thinks it could happen to them. Those are just stories you hear about from other businesses that have much looser IT security measures. Maybe you believe that your business isn't a target because it's too small or not the right industry. I'm here to tell you, sticking your head in the sand and convincing yourself you aren't a target is one of the very reasons there's a giant red target on your back.

While it may be difficult to determine the actual financial impact identity theft would have on your business, you can't deny the fact that it would have a negative effect. Cash most definitely is king. And if yours is stolen and used by a cybercriminal, the emotional toll such an event would take on you personally would certainly impact your business, even if you haven't put a pencil to figuring out the exact cost.

Here are some sobering statistics:

40% of consumers across the world have been targeted for identity theft.

There were 16.7 million identity theft victims in the US in 2017, resulting in the loss of $17 billion.

8 million records per day were stolen in just the first half of 2018, leading to 3.3 billion compromised data records.

HACK PROOF TIP

Create and implement a rapid response protocol for suspected identity theft or data breaches within your organization. This should include immediate steps for containment, assessment, notification, and remediation. By having a clear plan in place, you can act swiftly to minimize damage, engage with law enforcement if necessary, and start the recovery process.

Aside from the money and financial information and customer data potentially stolen, it's your time that you're truly being robbed of. And this statistic says it all: it takes the average victim of identity theft more than 600 hours to finally clear their name and clean up the fraud conducted with their personal information. Six hundred hours! That's the equivalent of nearly three months of working 40- hour workweeks! Can you afford to drop what you're doing and spend three months cleaning up this mess, getting your money back and defending your soiled name? Absolutely not. Nobody has that kind of time.

HACK PROOF CASE STUDY

Dr. Harper, Dental Clinic - A Dental Clinic's Defense Against Data Threats

Dr. Harper's dental clinic, a cornerstone of community health with a dedicated team of 15, including dentists, hygienists, and administrative staff, faced a daunting challenge when they realized their patient records were at risk of cyber intrusion. To safeguard their sensitive health information, we implemented Comprehensive Endpoint Threat Detection & Response, ensuring each computer and device was shielded against malware and cyber attacks. Additionally, we introduced a Suspicious Email Analysis Service (SEAS) to filter out phishing attempts, and initiated engaging Weekly Phishing Simulations to keep the entire team vigilant. This multi-faceted approach not only secured their patients' data but also reinforced the clinic's reputation as a trusted caretaker of both dental and digital health, ensuring the clinic could focus on smiles without the worry of data breaches.

Why Small Businesses Are More Vulnerable to Identity Theft

With the constant changes to technology and the daily development of new threats, it takes a highly trained technician to secure even a basic 5- to 10-person computer network. However, in an attempt to save money, many businesses try to do their own in-house IT support and designate the person with the most technical expertise as the part-time IT manager. This never works out because this makeshift IT person has another full-time job to do and is usually not skilled enough to properly support an entire computer network anyway.

This inevitably results in a network that is ill-maintained and unstable. It also means that the backups, virus updates and security patches are not getting timely updates, giving a false sense of security.

It's only a matter of time before an online hacker finds his way into your network and steals your information. If you're lucky, it will only cost you a little downtime, but there's always a chance you could end up like the companies affected by these criminals …

$764,000 Stolen from Insurance Company

A man was indicted, pleaded guilty to federal charges and was sentenced to 27 months' imprisonment for obtaining private bank account information about an insurance company's policyholders and using that information to deposit $764,000 in counterfeit checks into a bank account he established.

Social Security Number Swiped from a Website

A defendant has been indicted on bank fraud charges for obtaining names, addresses and social security numbers from a website and using the data to apply for a series of car loans over the Internet.

$13,000 Drained from This Business Owner's Account

A woman was indicted and pleaded guilty to federal charges involving her obtaining a fraudulent driver's license in the name of the victim, using the license to withdraw more than $13,000 from the victim's bank account and obtaining five department store credit cards in the victim's name and charging approximately $4,000 on those cards.

So, once these thieves steal your identity, what can they do with it? Well, in 2018, a Georgia man booked a three-night stay at a luxury Disney World hotel for $1,042. Next, he was very generous and bought 11 tickets to a Disney park at the hotel gift shop for a total of $1,582 (Mickey ain't cheap). On day two, he bought 11 more Disney tickets for nearly $2,000. Suspicious of the charges, officers detained the man and discovered he was carrying an Illinois driver's license and four credit cards that he purchased on the dark web! He attempted to give his family and friends a grand vacation on someone else's dime!

How Online Identity Thieves Get Hold of Your Information

Some identity theft does occur through more "old school" methods such as stealing your wallet, overhearing you give a credit card or social security number over the phone or even raiding your business filing cabinet or trash. However, common-sense tactics such as avoiding public conversations that involve your personal or business financial information or putting locks on your file cabinets can be used to combat those threats.

Internet threats to your identity, on the other hand, are much more sophisticated and involve greater "know-how" in order to prevent them.

There are four basic ways cybercriminals gain access to your personal information over the Internet. They are:

1. Phishing – Phishing is where online scammers send spam or pop-up messages to your computer and try to get you to provide personal or sensitive business information over the Internet. Online criminals will typically send messages that look like legitimate messages from your bank, credit card company or other financial institution. In the message, there is usually a website link where it asks you to update your contact information. Many

of these websites look like exact replicas of your bank or credit card website. However, entering your information into one of these sneaky portals means you are handing over the keys to the kingdom to a complete "evildoer". The Internet thief can now use your personal information to gain access to other private accounts, raid your business and rack up thousands of dollars in faulty charges.

2. Tech Support Scams – Scam artists are using the phone to try to break into your computer. They call, claiming to be computer techs associated with well-known companies like Microsoft. They say they have detected a virus or malware on your computer to trick you into giving them remote access or paying for software you don't need. The catch: these scammers take advantage of your reasonable concerns about viruses and other threats. They know that computer users have heard time and again that it's important to install security software. But the purpose behind their elaborate scheme isn't to protect your computer – it's to take money. They also may install remote tools on your devices to capture your data, copy your keystrokes and ultimately steal credit cards or login information.

3. Email Scams – Offers, detailed sales pitches, links to informational websites. These seemingly harmless

e-mails are actually the makings of an Internet crime. They'll ask for your credit card information to buy a fake product or to pay for shipping on a "free product." The most common email scams used to steal your identity are (as found on www.onguardonline.gov):

The "Nigerian" Email Scam. Con artists claim to be officials, businesspeople or the surviving spouses or former government honchos in Nigeria or another country whose money is somehow tied up for a limited time. They offer to transfer lots of money into your bank account if you will pay a fee or "taxes" to help them access their money. If you respond to the initial offer, you may receive documents that look "official." Then they ask you to send money to cover transaction and transfer costs and attorneys' fees, as well as blank letterhead, your bank account numbers or other information. They may even encourage you to travel to the country in question, or a neighboring country, to complete the transaction. Some fraudsters have even produced trucks of dyed or stamped money to try to verify their claims.

The Catch: The emails are from crooks trying to steal your money or your identity. Inevitably in this scenario, emergencies come up requiring more of your money and delaying the "transfer" of funds to your account. In the end, there aren't any profits for you, and the scam artist vanishes with your money. The harm sometimes can be felt even beyond your pocketbook: according to State Department reports, people who have responded to "pay in advance" solicitations have been beaten, subjected to threats and extortion and, in some cases, murdered.

Phishing Email Scam. E-mail or pop-up messages that claim to be from a business or organization you may deal with – say, an internet service provider (ISP), bank, online payment service or even a government agency. The message may ask you to "update," "validate" or "confirm" your account information or face dire consequences. One very popular scam occurs when the boss asks an employee to go buy Apple iTunes cards as client gifts and inadvertently sends the credit card details to the scammer. You could lose hundreds or even thousands of dollars!

The Catch: Phishing is a scam where Internet fraudsters send spam or pop-up messages to reel in personal and financial information from unsuspecting victims. The messages direct you to a website that looks just like a legitimate organization's site, or to a phone number purporting to be real. But these are bogus and exist simply to trick you into divulging your personal information so the operators can steal it, fake your identity and run up bills or commit crimes in your name.

4. **Spyware** – Spyware is software installed on your computer without your consent to monitor or control your computer use. Clues that spyware is on a computer may include a barrage of pop-ups, a browser that takes you to sketchy sites, unexpected toolbars or icons on your computer screen, keys that don't work, random error messages and sluggish performance when opening programs or saving files. In some cases, there may be no symptoms at all.

Four Ways to Protect Your Company from Identity Theft

While it's impossible to plan for every potential scenario, a little proactive planning and proper network precautions will help you avoid or greatly reduce the impact of the vast majority of cyber identity theft you could experience.

Step #1: Make Sure Your Backups Are Encrypted

It just amazes me how many businesses don't have the security of encrypted backups. Encryption takes every little keystroke that you type and every little piece of data in your computer and turns it into dozens – or hundreds – of other characters. For example, just one letter "A" could turn into 256 different letters, numbers and symbols when it is encrypted. It basically makes it a whole lot more difficult for a hacker to figure out what the data is. On the other hand, if you don't have encryption, you are opening yourself up to a big risk of your identity and other important data being swiped. That is why it is important to make sure your backup is properly secured.

Step #2: Make Sure Your Virus Protection Is Always On and Current

You would have to be living under a rock to not know how devastating a virus can be to your network. With virus attacks coming from spam, downloading data and music files, instant messages, websites and emails from friends and clients, you cannot afford to be without up-to-date virus protection.

Not only can a virus corrupt your files and bring down your network, it can also hurt your reputation. If you or one of your employees unknowingly spreads a virus to a customer, or if the virus hijacks your e-mail address book, you're going to make a lot of people very angry.

Step #3: Set Up a Firewall and Update It Regularly

Small-business owners tend to think that because they are "just a small business," no one would waste time trying to hack into their network, when nothing could be further from the truth. The simple fact is that there are thousands of unscrupulous individuals out there who think it's fun to steal your personal information just because they can. These individuals strike randomly by searching the Internet for open, unprotected ports. As soon as they find one, they will delete files or download huge files that cannot be deleted, shutting down your hard drive.They can also use your computer as a zombie for storing pirated software or sending spam, which will cause your ISP to shut you down and prevent you from accessing the Internet or sending and receiving e-mail.

If the malicious programs can't be deleted, you'll have to reformat the entire hard drive, causing you to lose every piece of information you've ever owned, unless you were backing up your files.

Step #4: Update Your System with Critical Security Patches as They Become Available

If you do not have the most up-to-date security patches and virus definitions installed on your network, hackers can access your computer through a simple banner ad or through an e-mail attachment.

HACK PROOF TIP

While implementing the protective measures outlined above, don't underestimate the power of continuous monitoring and rapid response! Ensure that your IT team or service provider conducts regular system audits and uses intrusion detection systems (IDS) to quickly spot unusual activities. By catching anomalies early, you can prevent potential breaches from escalating, safeguarding your company's and clients' data effectively.

Not too long ago, Microsoft released a security bulletin about three newly discovered vulnerabilities that could allow an attacker to gain control of your computer by tricking users into downloading and opening a maliciously crafted picture. At the same time, Microsoft released a Windows update to correct the vulnerabilities; but if you didn't have a process to ensure you were applying critical updates as soon as they became available, you were completely vulnerable to this attack. It is an easy way for someone to gain access to your information and steal your identity.

Here's another compelling reason to ensure your network stays up-to-date with the latest security patches. Most hackers do not discover these security loopholes on their own. Instead, they learn about them when Microsoft (or another software vendor) announces the vulnerability and issues an update. That is their cue to spring into action and they immediately go to work to analyze the update and craft an exploit (like a virus) that allows them access to any computer or network that has not yet installed the security patch.

In essence, the time between the release of the update and the release of the exploit that targets the underlying vulnerability is getting shorter every day.

By taking these proactive actions in your business, you are building a formidable defense against identity theft, one of today's most dangerous cyberattacks. Of course, if any of your employees work from home or on the road, there's a whole new world of potential security threats you may be up against. The next chapter will shine a light on the risks your business faces if employees are working from home, as well as what you can do now to mitigate those risks.

CHAPTER 9

Staying Secure While Working from Home

Key Takeaway: This chapter covers the key elements and risks that are inherent in remote work. Four detailed steps to take to ensure secure work-from-home environments.

Today more than ever before, business owners are taking advantage of a fast-growing trend among small and medium businesses that is drastically increasing productivity, cutting costs and driving more profit to the bottom line. Is it a new management style or marketing trend?

No – it's telecommuting, which is simply allowing your staff to work from home. When you see the bottom-line impact it has on profits and productivity and talk to business owners who rave about how much money it's saving them, you'll start to see how working from home is more than a necessity today – it's an opportunity.

Common Myths, Mistakes and Misconceptions about Allowing Your Employees to Work from Home

One of the most common fears many business owners have about allowing their team to work from home is the loss of control they have over their employees. Most think that unless someone is standing over them, employees will be unproductive and work far fewer hours.

But the proof says something entirely different. From 2005 to 2017, there was a 159% increase in remote work. Currently, more than 23 million people work from home at least one day a week. Not only does it save business owners in overhead, studies show that employees get MORE done when working outside of an office environment.

The Los Angeles Bank decided to test telecommuting to see if it would help their massive turnover rate of 33%. The experiment worked, and within a year the turnover rate plummeted to nearly zero. Not only were they able to pad their bottom line and flatten the turnover rate, their productivity jumped 18%, saving the bank more than $3 million each year.

AT&T allowed employees from a New Jersey office of 600 people to work from home. Over a five-year period, a region of AT&T saved more than $11 million annually. Half of those savings came from real estate savings while the other came from a measured increase in incremental work hours from employees who were now able to work without interruptions.

Even small businesses report savings of $85,000 to $93,000 per year by lowering their turnover rates, reducing their operating costs (gas, utilities, office space and furniture) and increased productivity after implementing work-from-home programs. (Source: International Teleworking Advocacy Group)

Cyber Security Risks for Telecommuters

While there's clear evidence today of the many benefits of allowing your team to work from home, those benefits come at a heightened risk to your network and data. Remote work can present a unique challenge because work-from-home environments usually don't have the same level of cyber security found within your office.

Here are six of the top cyber security risks you should be cautious of when implementing a work-from-home team.

1. Public WiFi – From Starbucks to libraries to doctors' waiting rooms, public WiFi seems to be just about everywhere nowadays. While it's convenient to just hop on a public WiFi, it poses significant security risks to your network. First, other people have access to that same network, and without a

firewall between you and them, there's potential for someone nearby accessing the same data that you can. Second, any interested observers on your current network or the public networks can monitor your traffic since it's not encrypted.

2. Personal Computers and Devices – When your staff is working from home, it may be more convenient for them to use their home PC or devices to run reports, send e-mails or even access your network. You and your IT team have probably gone to great lengths to ensure your work computers have the latest updates installed, run antivirus scans and block malicious sites. However, most business owners and IT staff rarely follow the same security procedures for personal computers and devices, such as ensuring the work device has the Windows firewall enabled to protect it from other home computers and Internet of Things (IoT) devices.

   Essentially, by introducing a personal computer to a work network, even remotely, you're putting the company network and your business at unnecessary risk. Even beyond the risk to your data is the potential liability and financial risk through violations of policy, practices or both.

3. Risk of Theft – While you know there's a threat of cybercriminals hacking your network and stealing

your data, you probably rarely think about someone stealing the computers in your office. However, because laptops and tablets are portable and much easier to steal, there is a greater chance of theft.

Advise your employees to never leave their work computers or devices in a vehicle or unattended in a restaurant. It only takes a few seconds for someone to break into your car or even the trunk and take a laptop. While on the road, it's smarter to always keep your laptop on your person. Because a stolen laptop means a lot worse than simply replacing a computer, it can also be a productivity and records nightmare. The worst- case scenario? The theft is actually a hacker who is after the personal data and passwords left on the laptop

4. Flash Drives – Your IT team goes to such great lengths to keep your network safe. And it can all be brought down by a cheap little thumb drive or flash drive. Most families have several of these portable drives in random desk drawers and kids' rooms. If an employee picks up a random thumb drive, it's like playing Russian roulette – will it contain malware or not? A classic hacking technique is to drop off several thumb drives at an office or public location. Most people will appreciate the free drive and take it home for future use. By doing so, they could possibly unleash a virus or malware onto

the computer and possibly even your network!

In a study presented at a hacker conference, a Google researcher dropped off 297 USB drives in hallways, parking lots and outdoor areas on the University of Illinois's Urbana-Champaign campus. Inside the drives was special software that would allow them to immediately "call home" when plugged in. Of the 297 USB drives, 98% were picked up and 45% were plugged in and called home! Bottom line: never use a flash drive if you don't know what's on it and who gave it to you.

5. Sending Sensitive Information Via E-mail – Your remote employees won't think twice about sending emails either from their work computer or their personal laptop. However, when you're sending sensitive data, such as financial information, passwords or proprietary product information, there's always a chance it could be intercepted by a third party. Encrypting the data attached to an email prevents an unintended recipient from intercepting and viewing the data. Also, be sure your device is set to have all stored data encrypted in case of theft.

6. People Are Watching – You've already been warned about using public WiFi. There's another risk if you're in a public place doing work. It's other people. If you're in a coffee shop, you should always be

aware of your sight lines. Anyone behind you can see everything you're typing. Cybercriminals have strong observational skills to easily watch what you are doing and steal confidential information.

Four Steps to Take to Ensure Secure Work-from- Home Environments

Now that you better understand the cyber security risks of allowing your team to work from home, we want to give you the tools, technologies and insights into creating a more productive remote business environment. Here are four considerations to getting you set up and running a productive and protected work- from-home business.

Step 1: Use Two-Factor Authentication VPN

VPN stands for virtual private network. It's essentially a private, encrypted tunnel that goes direct to your IT network in your office. Ideally, you'll want your VPN to support two-factor authentication. This means that it's doubly secure because your employees will need to call in to access the network.

Ideally, your employees would be accessing corporate resources through a VPN remote access rather than a cloud-based "virtual desktop" solution, such as GoToMyPC or Zoho. These products are not as secure, but they are still better than not using anything and exposing your network to risk.

Step 2: Use a Secure WiFi Access Point

Without a secure WiFi access point, you're essentially leaving a back door open to hackers. That's because WiFi signals are often broadcast far beyond your employees' homes and out into the streets. Yes, drive-by hacking is popular among cybercriminals today.

A few tips for using a secure WiFi access point: First, use a stronger encryption and a more complex password. Second, hide your network name so your neighbors or people in your proximity cannot see your network. Third, use a firewall.

Step 3: Improve Your Password Strategy

The strength of your passwords may be the first line of defense that shields against would-be hackers. Make a point to reevaluate your passwords and inform your team to create stronger passwords. While it's convenient to save your passwords in a web browser, it also lessens your security. Because web browsers simply require their own password or PIN to access saved passwords, a skilled hacker can bypass this hurdle. Once they access your saved passwords, they can steal as much as they want – credit card information, customers' private data and more.

Another tip is to never use the same password for more than one account or website. Too many people utilize one password for all of their accounts.

If that single password ever gets leaked, ALL of their accounts are compromised. Instead, by using different passwords, you only have to change the one password on the compromised website or software.

To make it far easier to deal with multiple passwords, you should consider a password manager to keep all of your passwords in one place. These password managers feature robust security.

Step 4: Provide Company-Approved Computers

You have practically zero control regarding what's on your employees' home computers and who is using them. That same computer they access your network with could be used to download music and apps, play video games, surf controversial sites and receive potentially dangerous emails.

While it may seem like an added expense to issue company- approved computers or laptops to all of your work-from-home employees, the investment could prevent a much more serious cyberattack that could cost your business far more. Many business owners today are providing their employees laptops rather than PCs and monitors so they can easily take them home. Just make sure they protect their company laptop and never leave it in their car or unattended in a public place.

Whether your employees are currently working from home or you're considering the benefits of letting them work remotely, apply these tips to help protect your team, their computers and your network and data.

HACK PROOF TIP

Consider implementing geofencing technology to add an extra layer of security for your remote workforce. Geofencing can restrict access to sensitive company data to specific geographical locations. For example, employees can only access certain company resources when they are within the predefined safe zones, like their home or designated workspaces. This technology not only protects against external threats but also helps in controlling data access based on location, significantly reducing the risk of data breaches when devices are outside secured areas.

CHAPTER 10

Is Your Current IT Company Doing Their Job?

Take This Quiz to Find Out

Cybersecurity Self-Assessment Questionnaire

To accompany your journey through Hack Proof we have developed a concise self-assessment questionnaire. This tool is designed to provide you with a snapshot of your current cybersecurity posture and identify areas for improvement. By answering the following questions, you'll gain insights into how well your business is protected against potential cyber threats.

Instructions:

- Read each question carefully and answer honestly based on your current practices. You can answer the questions right in the book or scan the QR code to take the quiz online.

- At the end of the questionnaire, tally your scores according to the scoring guide provided.
- Use your score to assess your cybersecurity posture and identify areas for improvement.

Scan the QR code to access the quiz.

Questionnaire - Is Your Current IT Company Doing Their Job?

1. Do you have an active antivirus and anti-malware solution installed on all devices?
    - Yes (2 points)
    - No (0 points)

2. Is your software, including operating systems and applications, regularly updated?
    - Yes (2 points)
    - No (0 points)

3. Do you use multi-factor authentication (MFA) for accessing sensitive systems and data?
    - Yes (2 points)
    - No (0 points)

4. Have you conducted a cybersecurity risk assessment in the past year?
    - Yes (2 points)
    - No (0 points)

5. Do you have a formal cybersecurity policy in place that is communicated to all employees?
    - Yes (2 points)
    - No (0 points)

6. Are regular cybersecurity training and awareness programs conducted for employees?
   - Yes (2 points)
   - No (0 points)

7. Do you regularly back up data and have a recovery plan in case of a cyber incident?
   - Yes (2 points)
   - No (0 points)

8. Do you encrypt sensitive data both in transit and at rest?
   - Yes (2 points)
   - No (0 points)

9. Do you have an incident response plan that is regularly tested?
   - Yes (2 points)
   - No (0 points)

10. Do you regularly review and manage the access rights of employees to systems and data?
    - Yes (2 points)
    - No (0 points)

Scoring Guide:

- 18-20 points: Excellent - Your cybersecurity

practices are strong, but always look for areas to improve.

- 10-17 points: Good - You have a solid foundation, but there are several areas you can enhance to better protect your business.
- 0-9 points: Needs Improvement - Your cybersecurity practices need significant enhancement. Consider prioritizing this to protect your business.

Next Steps:

Based on your score, review the areas where you can improve your cybersecurity posture. Remember, cybersecurity is an ongoing process. Regularly reassess your practices and stay informed on the latest threats and protection strategies.

If your current IT company does not score a "Yes" on every point, they are not adequately protecting you. Don't let them "convince" you otherwise and do not give them a free pass on any one of these critical points.

Further, it's important that you get verification on the items listed. Simply asking, "Do you have insurance to cover us if you make a mistake?" is not sufficient. Protecting your business by having a paper trail of the conversation, and getting a copy of the policy or other verification is critical. When it comes down to it, they can deny they told you.

Checklist of Questions to Ask Your IT Security Team

- ☐ Have they met with you recently – in the last three months – to specifically review and discuss what they are doing now to protect you? Have they told you about new and inexpensive tools such as dark web monitoring for your company's credentials or advanced endpoint security to protect you from attacks that antivirus is unable to detect and prevent?
- ☐ If you are outsourcing your IT support, they should, at a minimum, provide you with a quarterly review and report of what they've done – and are doing – to protect you AND to discuss new threats and areas you will need to address.
- ☐ Do they proactively monitor, patch and update your computer network's critical security settings? Is the frequency daily, weekly or at all? Are they reviewing your firewall's event logs for suspicious activity? How do you know for sure? Are they providing any kind of verification to you or your team?
- ☐ Have they recommended you to talk to your insurance company to make sure you have the

right kind of insurance to protect against fraud or cyber liability?

- ☐ Do they have adequate insurance to cover you if they make a mistake and your network is compromised? Do you have a copy of their current policy? Does it specifically cover YOU for losses and damages? You should ask if they have an Errors-and-Omissions (E&O) insurance policy, as well as a cyber liability policy.
- ☐ Have you been fully and frankly briefed on what to do if you get compromised? Have they provided you with a response plan? If not, WHY NOT?
- ☐ Have they told you if they are outsourcing your support to a third party? Do you know who has access to your personal computer and network? If they are outsourcing, have they shown you what security controls they have in place to ensure a rogue technician, living in another country, would be prevented from using their free and full access to your network to do harm?
- ☐ Have they kept their technicians trained on new cyber security threats and technologies, rather than just winging it? Do they have anyone on staff experienced in conducting security risk assessments? Does their business have key partnerships with today's most prominent IT vendors?

- ☐ Do they have a ransomware-proof backup system in place? One of the reasons the WannaCry virus was so devastating was because it was designed to find, corrupt and lock BACKUP files as well. Ask them to verify this. You might think you have it because that's what your IT vendor is telling you.
- ☐ Have they put in place a written mobile and remote device security policy, and distributed it to you and your employees? Is the data encrypted on these devices? Do you have a remote "kill" switch that would wipe the data from a lost or stolen device, and is that data backed up so you can wipe the device and not lose files?
- ☐ Do they have controls in place to force your employees to use strong passwords? Do they require a 90-day password update for all employees that falls within the National Institute of Standards and Technology? If an employee is fired or quits, do they have a process in place to make sure all passwords are changed? Can you see it?
- ☐ Have they talked to you about replacing your old antivirus with advanced endpoint security? There has been considerable talk in the IT industry that antivirus is dead, unable to prevent the sophisticated attacks we're seeing today.
- ☐ Have they discussed and/or implemented "multi-factor authentication" for access to highly sensitive

data? Do you even know what that is? If not, you don't have it.

- ☐ Have they recommended or conducted a comprehensive risk assessment every single year? Many insurance policies require it to cover you in the event of a breach. If you handle "sensitive data" such as medical records, credit card and financial information, social security numbers, etc., you may be required by law to do this.
- ☐ Have they implemented web-filtering technology to prevent your employees from going to infected websites, or websites you don't want them accessing at work? Porn and adult content is still the #1 searched content online. This can expose you to sexual harassment and child pornography lawsuits, not to mention the distraction and time wasted on your dime, with your company-owned equipment.
- ☐ Have they given you and your employees any kind of cyber security awareness training? Have they offered to help you create an AUP (acceptable use policy)? Employees accidentally clicking on a phishing email, downloading an infected file or malicious application is still the #1 way cybercriminals hack into systems. Training your employees frequently is one of the most important protections you can put into place.
- ☐ Have they implemented random phishing emails

to test your employees? There's no better education than real-life scenarios. Of course, if they fail the phishing tests, those employees should attend additional training.

- ☐ Have they properly configured your email system to prevent the sending/receiving of confidential or protected data? Properly configured email systems can automatically prevent emails containing specific data, like social security numbers, from being sent or received.
- ☐ Do they allow your employees to connect remotely using GoToMyPC, LogMeIn or TeamViewer? This is a sure sign to be concerned. Remote access should strictly be via a secure VPN (virtual private network).
- ☐ Do they offer, or have they at least talked to you about, dark web/deep web ID monitoring? There are new tools available that monitor cybercrime websites and data for your specific credentials being sold or traded. Once these are detected, it notifies you immediately so you can change your password and be on high alert.
- ☐ Do they offer a Security Information and Event Management (SIEM) solution to ensure unwanted traffic isn't coming from within your own network? SIEM software is critical in today's security world because it can detect and log as many as 25,000 events per second.

CONCLUSION

As we navigate through the digital age, the importance of cybersecurity in protecting our businesses and personal lives cannot be overstated. The inspiration to write "HACK PROOF" stemmed from my experiences in the field of cybersecurity and the realization that, despite its critical importance, many remain unaware or underprepared for the digital threats that loom over us.

Throughout my career in managing an MSP and Cybersecurity company, I've witnessed firsthand the devastation that cyber-attacks can bring to unsuspecting businesses—ranging from financial loss to irreparable damage to reputation. This book is born out of a desire to bridge the gap between complex cybersecurity concepts and practical, actionable strategies that businesses of all sizes can implement.

Now that you have turned the final pages of this book, I hope you see that cybersecurity is not a destination, but a journey. The landscape of digital threats is ever evolving, and so too must our defenses. I encourage you to approach this journey with curiosity, vigilance, and the willingness to continuously learn and adapt.

GLOSSARY

Technical Terms in Plain English

Key Takeaway: A comprehensive glossary of technical terms that will enable you to process the information you need and to be able to explain to IT teams when you have issues.

Too often, IT services providers "hide" behind acronyms and technical terms. By making technology harder to understand, they keep themselves in a position of being valuable and necessary. After all, the less you understand, the more you depend on them.

Everyone on our team has the heart of a teacher. We believe you should understand your computers and network because they contain your important data. Therefore, we always strive to educate and inform whenever possible. If you're ever confused or questioning why your IT consultant is recommending a product, service or strategy, please ask them. If they dismiss your questions, they are salespeople – not teachers – at heart.

In an effort to be as transparent as possible, we've included plain English definitions for some of today's more common technology terms.

Access Point – A device that allows wireless-equipped computers and other devices to communicate with a wired network.

ASP: Application Service Provider – A third-party company that manages and distributes software-based services and solutions to their customers over a wide-area network, usually the Internet.

Authentication – The process of identifying yourself and the verification that you're who you say you are. Computers where restricted information is stored may require you to enter your username and password to gain access.

BYOD: Bring Your Own Device – A business and technology policy that allows employees to bring in personal mobile devices and use these devices to access company data, e-mail, etc.

Cloud Computing – Internet-based computing, whereby shared resources, software and information are provided to computers and other devices on demand, as with the electricity grid.

Content Filtering – Software that prevents users from accessing or sending questionable content via your Internet. Content filtering is used to block job application sites, dating sites, gambling sites, shopping sites, as well as pornography, explicit language and images. Many programs also screen inbound and outbound emails for offensive and confidential information. This software is not designed for virus, worm or hacker prevention.

CPU: Central Processing Unit – The brains of a computer.

CSP: Cloud Service Provider – A business model for providing cloud services.

Dark Web – The unknown, hidden part of the web that consists of websites that use the public Internet, but requires specific software for access and is not indexed by search engines. Stolen data on the dark web is traded, sold and used for financial or political gain.

Deep Web – Ninety percent of the web is actually the deep web, just below the surface of the World Wide Web. Web developers and companies tell Google not to index the information so it's not searchable.

Default Gateway – In a TCP/IP network, this is the gateway that computers on that network use to send data to, and receive it from, computers and networks outside of the local network. Typically, this is the router or firewall that connects the local network to the public Internet, although it might also be a router that connects to another remote server or computer within the same company.

DHCP: Dynamic Host Configuration Protocol – A method for dynamically assigning IP addresses to devices on request, rather than explicitly programming an IP address into each device. If you have a server on your network, configuring that server as a DHCP server will make it much easier to add or reconfigure individual workstations on the network.

DMZ: Demilitarized Zone – A separate area of your network that is isolated from both the Internet and your protected internal network. A DMZ is usually created by your firewall to provide a location for devices such as web servers that you want to be accessible from the public Internet.

DNS: Domain Name Server (or Server) – An Internet service that translates domain names into IP addresses. Even though most domain names are alphabetic, hardware devices (like your PC) can only send data to a specific IP address. When you type www.microsoft.

com into your web browser, or send an e-mail message to someone@business.com, your web browser and e-mail server have to be able to look up the IP address that corresponds to the microsoft.com web server, or to the mail server that receives email for business.com. DNS is the mechanism for doing this lookup.

EHR/EMR/PHR: Electronic Health Record/Electronic Health Record/Personal Health Record – These terms are used interchangeably to refer to record patient-centered health records.

Encryption – The manipulation of data to prevent accurate interpretation by all but those for whom the data is intended.

Endpoint Protection – Also referred to as endpoint security, it's an approach to detecting malicious activity while protecting secure networks, including servers, computers and devices from an attack.

Ethernet – Ethernet is the standard wired network technology in use almost everywhere today. If your computer is connected to a network via a cable, it's likely using an Ethernet cable. That cable plugs into an Ethernet port on your computer.

Firewall – A device or software program designed to protect your network from unauthorized access over the Internet. It may also provide network address translation (NAT) and virtual private network (VPN) functionally.

Hosted Applications (e.g., Hosted Sharepoint or Hosted Exchange) – A service whereby a provider makes a software (e.g., e-mail) and space available on a server so its clients can host their data on that server.

IaaS: Infrastructure as a Service – In the most basic cloud- service model, providers of IaaS offer computers – physical or (more often) virtual machines – and other resources.

ISP: Internet Service Provider – Your Internet service provider is the company that provides you with your Internet connection. For example, your ISP may be Comcast, Time Warner or whatever other company you're paying each month.

LAN: Local Area Network – A small network that's confined to a local area. For example, your home network or an office network is a LAN. A LAN connects a group of computers for the purpose of sharing resources such as programs, documents or printers. Shared files often are stored on a central file server.

Mail Server – A networked computer dedicated to supporting electronic mail. You use a client program like Microsoft Outlook for retrieving new mail from the server and for composing and sending messages.

Microsoft Exchange Server – The server side of a client server, collaborative application product developed by Microsoft. It is part of the Microsoft Servers line of server products and is used by enterprises using Microsoft infrastructure products. Exchange's major features consist of e-mail, calendaring, contacts and tasks; support for mobile and web-based access to information; and support for data storage.

MSP: Managed Services Provider – A proactive and responsive business model for providing information-technology services. A managed services provider can save you considerable money by minimizing costly network disasters while decreasing downtime by providing proactive solutions. By ensuring your network and data are secure, reliable and running just as it should, MSPs provide peace of mind.

Multi-Factor Authentication – An authentication method in which a computer user is granted access only after successfully presenting two or more pieces of evidence to an authentication mechanism: knowledge, possession and inherence. Two-factor authentication is a type, or subset, or multi-factor authentication.

Nameserver – A computer that runs a program for converting Internet domain names into the corresponding IP addresses and vice versa.

Network Interface/Network Adapter – Your computer's wired Ethernet connection and WiFi connection are basically both network interfaces. If your laptop was connected to both a wired connection and a WiFi network, each network interface would have its own IP address. Each is a different connection.

Next-Generation Endpoint Security – Beyond traditional endpoint security solutions, next-generation endpoint security utilizes modern artificial intelligence and machine learning to provide real-time analysis of user and system behavior. These advanced tools address threats and also learn from threats and continuously adapt methods and combat them with greater speed and efficiency.

Patch – Piece of software designed to update a computer program or its supporting data, to fix or improve it. This includes fixing security vulnerabilities and other bugs, and improving the usability or performance.

Port – When an application wants to send or receive traffic, it has to use a numbered port between 1 to 65535. This is how you can have multiple applications on a computer using the network and each application knows which traffic is for it.

Protocol – An agreed format for transmitting data between two devices. TCP and UDP are the most common protocols. The ICMP protocol is also used, but primarily so network devices can check each other's status. Different protocols are ideal for different types of communication.

Remote Desktop – A Windows feature that allows you to have access to a Windows session from another computer in a different location.

Remote Login – An interactive connection from your desktop computer over an Internet connection to a computer at a remote site.

RMM: Remote Monitoring and Management – A piece of software managed services providers use to monitor the performance of endpoints and other IT assets remotely. From a single device, you can monitor systems, remotely access devices, review data, deploy patches and more.

Router – A device used for connecting two local area networks (LANs); a device that passes traffic back and forth. You likely have a home router. The router's job is to pass outgoing traffic from your local devices to the Internet and to pass incoming traffic from the Internet to your devices. A router is also used if you have multiple office locations and you need all devices to communicate to the home office servers.

SaaS: Software as a Service – A software distribution model in which a third-party provider hosts applications and makes them available to customers over the Internet. SaaS is one of three main categories of cloud computing, alongside infrastructure as a service (IaaS) and platform as a service (PaaS).

SAN: Storage Area Network – A dedicated storage network that provides access to consolidated, block level storage. SANs are primarily used to make storage devices accessible to servers so the devices appear as locally attached to the operating system. A SAN typically has its own network of storage devices that are generally not accessible through the regular network by regular devices.

SIEM: Security Information and Event Management – A software solution that aggregates and analyzes activity from many different resources across your IT network. SIEM collects security from network devices, servers and more.

SMTP: Simple Mail Transfer Protocol – An Internet standard for e-mail transmission.

SOC: Security Operations Center – A centralized unit that deals with security issues on an organizational and technical level. A SOC within a building or facility is a central location from which staff supervises the site, using data processing technology. Typically, a SOC is equipped for device monitoring such as hacker threats.

Spam – Email spam, also known as junk e-mail or unsolicited bulk e-mail, is a subset of spam that involves nearly identical messages sent to numerous recipients by email. By definition, spam is unsolicited and sent in bulk. Spammers collect email addresses from chatrooms, websites, newsgroups and viruses that harvest users' address books and are sold to other spammers.

Spear Phishing – Phishing attempt directed at specific individuals or companies. In contrast to bulk phishing, spear phishing attackers often gather and use personal information about their target to increase the probability of successfully getting their victim to take action.

SSL: Secure Socket Layer – Small data files that digitally bind a cryptographic key to an organization's details. When installed on a web server, it activates the padlock and the HTTPS protocol and allows secure connections from a web server to a browser. Typically, SSL is used to secure credit card transactions, data transfer and logins, and more recently is becoming the norm when securing browsing of social media sites.

Switch – Serves as a controller, enabling networked devices to talk to each other efficiently. Through information-sharing and resource allocation, switches save businesses money and increase employee productivity.

TCP/IP: Transmission Control Protocol/Internet Protocol – An agreed-upon set of rules that tells computers how to exchange information over the Internet. Other Internet protocols, like FTP, Gopher and HTTP, sit on top of TCP/IP.

Threat Actor – Any individual or group of individuals who attempt to conduct malicious activities against enterprises. Threat actors can be internal or external.

Two-Factor Authentication – An extra level of security achieved using a security token device; users have a personal identification number (PIN) that identifies them as the owner of a particular token. The token displays a number that is entered following the PIN number to uniquely identify the owner of a particular network service. The identification number for each user is changed frequently, usually every few minutes.

URL: Uniform Resource Locator – The global address of documents, websites and other resources on the web.

Virus – A program intended to alter data on a computer in an invisible fashion, usually for mischievous or destructive purposes. Viruses are often transferred across the Internet, as well as by infected diskettes, and can affect almost every type of computer. Special antivirus programs are used to detect and eliminate them.

VoIP: Voice over Internet Protocol – A means of using the Internet as the transmission medium for phone calls. An advantage is you do not incur any additional surcharges beyond the cost of the Internet access.

VPN: Virtual Private Network – A network constructed by using public wires (the Internet) to connect nodes (usually computers and servers). A VPN uses encryption and other security mechanisms to ensure that only authorized users can access the network and the data it holds. This allows businesses to connect to other servers and computers located in remote offices, from home or while traveling.

WAN: Wide Area Network – A larger network used to connect two or more locations. If you have two or more offices and want to send and receive data securely between them, a WAN is ideal.

WAP: Wireless Application Protocol – A set of communication protocols for enabling wireless access to the Internet.

WEP: Wired Equivalent Privacy – A security protocol for wireless local area networks defined in the 802.11b used in a wireless network. WEP provides the same level of security as that of a wired LAN.

WiFi: Wireless Fidelity – A generic term from the WiFi Alliance that refers to any type of 802.11

network. Products approved as "WiFi Certified" are certified as interoperable with each other for wireless communications.

WLAN: Wireless Local Area Network – The computers and devices that make up a wireless network.

WPA: WiFi Protected Access – A standard designed to improve on the security features of WEP.

HACK PROOF BOOK BONUS

A Free Cyber Security Risk Assessment

As readers of this book you are eligible to receive a free Cyber Security Risk Assessment from our team.

A security assessment is the only way you can be really sure of your IT Security for your online business. The process is exactly what it sounds like – it can review, evaluate and "stress test" your company's network to uncover loopholes and vulnerabilities before a cyber event happens.

Just like a cancer screening, a good assessment can catch problems while they're small, which means they will be alot less expensive to fix, less disruptive to your organization and give you a better chance of surviving a cyberattack.

An assessment should always be done by a qualified

third party, not your current IT team or company; fresh eyes see things hidden, even in plain sight, from those looking at it on a daily basis.

You want a qualified "Sherlock Holmes" investing on YOUR behalf who is not trying to cover up inadequacies or make excuses; bringing to you a confidential report you can see and understand.

Our Free Cyber Security Risk Assessment Will Give You the Answers You Want, and the Certainty You Need.

For a limited time, we are offering a complimentary Cyber Security Risk Assessment to our readers of Hack Proof. This is entirely free and without obligation. Everything we find and everything discussed will be strictly confidential.

This assessment will provide verification from a qualified third party on whether or not your current IT company is doing everything they should to keep your computer network not only up and running, but safe from cybercrime.

Here's How It Works: At no cost or obligation, one of our cybersecurity consultants will conduct a remote, non-invasive, confidential investigation of your computer network, backups and security protocols. Your current IT company or person does not need to know we are conducting this assessment. Your time investment is minimal: one hour for the initial meeting and one hour in the second meeting to discuss our Report of Findings.

When this Risk Assessment is complete, you will know:

If your login credentials and your employees' are being sold on the dark web. We will run a scan on your company, right in front of you, in the privacy of your office if you prefer (results will not be e-mailed or otherwise shared with anyone but you). It's rare that we don't find compromised credentials – and I can guarantee what we find will shock and alarm you.

If your IT systems and data are truly secured from hackers, cybercriminals, viruses, worms and even sabotage by rogue employees.

If your current backup would allow you to be back up and running again fast if ransomware locked all your files. In far too many of the computer networks we've reviewed over the years, the owners were shocked to learn the backup they had would NOT survive a ransomware attack.

If employees truly know how to spot a phishing email. We will actually put them to the test. We've never seen a company pass 100%. Not once.

If we do find problems ... overlooked security loopholes, inadequate backups, credentials that have been compromised, out- of-date firewall and antivirus software and (often) active malware... on one or more of the PCs in your office, we will propose an Action

Plan to remediate the situation that you can have us implement for you if you choose.

Why is this assessment free?

Frankly, we want the opportunity to be your IT and Cybersecurity company. We know we are one of the most competent, responsive and trusted IT services providers to small businesses in North America.

However, I also realize there's a good chance you've been burned, disappointed and frustrated by the complete lack of service and the questionable advice you've gotten from other IT companies in the past. In fact, you might be so fed up and disgusted with being "sold" and underserved that you don't trust anyone. I don't blame you.

That's why this assessment is completely and entirely free. Let us earn your trust by demonstrating our expertise. While we would love the opportunity to be your IT company, we will come in with no expectations and only look to provide you with fact-based information so you can make a quality, informed decision – and we'll only discuss the option of becoming your IT company if the information we share makes sense and you want to move forward. No hard sell. No gimmicks and no tricks.

Please ... Do Not Just Shrug This Off (What To Do Now)

You've spent a lifetime working hard to get where you are today.

Get the facts and be certain you are protected.

Contact us and schedule your free, confidential Cyber Security Risk Assessment today at https://CapitalTek.com. Feel free to also reach out to me direct at 613-227-4357 x 200 or e-mail: sergey@capitaltek.com

AUTHOR'S NOTE

My journey in writing HACK PROOF - A Guide to Cybersecurity for Your Business was both challenging and enlightening. I've had the privilege of engaging with some of the brightest minds in cybersecurity, whose insights and expertise have greatly influenced the content of this book. It was my goal to distill these complex topics into understandable and applicable advice that can fortify your business against cyber threats.

Thank you for choosing to embark on this important journey with me. Together, let's take proactive steps to safeguard our digital world.

Warm regards,
Sergey

ACKNOWLEDGEMENTS

As this book reaches publication, I am reminded that the journey of writing "HACK PROOF A Guide to Cybersecurity for Your Business" has been as much about collaboration and support as it has been about the solitary pursuit of writing. It is with deep gratitude that I acknowledge the many people who have made this book possible.

First and foremost, I extend my sincere thanks to my colleagues at CapitalTek whose expertise and insights into the nuances of cybersecurity have been invaluable. Your dedication to protecting our digital frontiers is the bedrock upon which this book is built.

I am especially grateful to my mom who bought me my first computer when I was 12 because this is what got me into IT and eventually Cybersecurity, for believing in me and steering me to get a Computer Degree.

To the cybersecurity community at large, thank

you for your relentless pursuit of safety and security in an ever-evolving digital landscape. The research, discussions, and shared knowledge from this community have been critical in shaping the perspectives presented in this book.

To my family and friends, for your patience, understanding, and unwavering support, I am eternally grateful. Your encouragement during the inevitable challenges of this project has been a source of strength and motivation.

And finally, to you, the readers, who recognize the critical importance of cybersecurity in protecting our businesses and personal lives. This book is for you—may it empower you with the knowledge and strategies to navigate the complex world of cybersecurity.

Thank you all for being part of this journey. Together, we can make a difference in creating a safer digital world for everyone.

~ Sergey

MEET SERGEY POLTEV

Founder & CEO of CapitalTek

From the resilience of a youth in a small Russian town to the forefront of cybersecurity in Canada, Sergey's journey is a testament to the power of determination and innovation. Facing the void left by his father's untimely death, Sergey stepped up to become the pillar of strength for his family. His fascination with technology, sparked at the mere age of twelve, led him to transform a personal computer into a beacon of hope and opportunity.

Armed with ambition and a Computer Science degree, Sergey relocated to Ottawa, Canada and founded CapitalTek in 2005 where he continued to grow his expertise based on his foundation in networking, cybersecurity, and IT management. 26 years of hands-on experience make him the ideal champion of cybersecurity. He and CapitalTek stand guard over small businesses, protecting them from the pervasive dangers of the cyber world, including ransomware, malware, and identity theft that threaten billions of accounts annually.

Dedicated to enabling businesses to focus on their strengths, Sergey and his team became the unsung heroes during the Covid-19 pandemic, architecting vital work-from-home solutions for local businesses. His strategic foresight and practical solutions continue to guide companies through times of crisis and change.

Now, as the leader of CapitalTek, an IT Company in Canada, Sergey safeguards businesses against the digital underworld. His story is not just about combating cyber threats but also about empowering others with the skills to thrive in an ever-evolving technological landscape.

Sergey is passionate about helping businesses focus on what they do best without having to worry about their computer systems.

Let's Connect

Email - sergey@capitaltek.com
Phone - +1-613-227- 4357 x 200

Online

https://hackproofbook.com
https://capitaltek.com
https://www.linkedin.com/company/capitaltek
https://www.facebook.com/CapitalTek/

RECOMMENDED READING

"The Art of Deception: Controlling the Human Element of Security" by Kevin D. Mitnick - A compelling read from one of the world's most famous former hackers, this book delves into the human factors of cybersecurity and how social engineering can be used to breach security systems. Mitnick's insights are invaluable for business owners looking to understand and defend against these types of attacks.

"Cybersecurity and Cyberwar: What Everyone Needs to Know®" by P.W. Singer and Allan Friedman - This accessible guide provides a thorough overview of cybersecurity's key issues and challenges. It's an excellent primer for business owners who want to understand the complexities of cyber threats in the modern world.

"Data and Goliath: The Hidden Battles to Collect Your Data and Control Your World" by Bruce Schneier -

Schneier explores the far-reaching implications of mass data collection and surveillance. This book is crucial for understanding the privacy concerns businesses must navigate in today's digital landscape.

"Future Crimes: Everything Is Connected, Everyone Is Vulnerable and What We Can Do About It" by Marc Goodman - Offering a look into the digital future, Goodman discusses how emerging technologies can pose new threats to businesses. This book is a wake-up call to the evolving landscape of cybercrime.

"Hacking Leadership: The 11 Gaps Every Business Needs to Close and the Secrets to Closing Them Quickly" by Mike Myatt - While not strictly about cybersecurity, this book addresses leadership gaps that can indirectly affect a company's security posture. It's an essential read for business owners looking to lead more effectively and create a culture of security.

"Playing to the Edge: American Intelligence in the Age of Terror" by Michael V. Hayden - Hayden provides insight into the practices of American intelligence agencies in the post-9/11 world, offering lessons on risk management and decision-making that are applicable to cybersecurity strategies for businesses.

"Cybersecurity for Beginners" by Raef Meeuwisse - This book breaks down complex cybersecurity concepts into understandable segments, perfect for business owners new to the subject. It covers the basics of cybersecurity practices and how to implement them effectively.

"Cult of the Dead Cow: How the Original Hacking Supergroup Might Just Save the World" by Joseph Menn - An intriguing look at one of the oldest hacking groups and its impact on cybersecurity. This book offers perspective on the ethical dilemmas and challenges in securing the digital world, relevant for business owners navigating cybersecurity ethics.

BIBLIOGRAPHY

CSO Online. (n.d.). Fraud Prevention: Heartland pays Amex $3.6 million over 2008 data breach.

https://www.csoonline.com/article/524390/fraud-prevention-heartland-pays-amex-3-6-million-over-2008-data-breach.html

Lewis, D. (2015, May 31). Heartland Payment Systems Suffers Data Breach. Forbes.

https://www.forbes.com/sitesdavelewis/2015/05/31/heartland-payment-systems-suffers-data-breach/?sh=5ec33c9e744a

CNET. (n.d.). Adobe hack attack affected 38 million accounts.

https://www.cnet.com/news/privacy/adobe-hack-attack-affected-38-million-accounts/

BBC News. (2013, November 7). Adobe hack attack affected 38 million accounts.

https://www.bbc.com/news/technology-24740873

Business Insider. (2014, May 21). Cyber thieves took data on 145 million eBay customers by hacking 3 corporate employees.

https://www.businessinsider.com/cyber-thieves-took-data-on-145-million-ebay-customers-by-hacking-3-corporate-employees-2014-5

USA Today. (2014, November 6). Home Depot Hackers Stolen Data.

https://www.usatoday.com/story/money/business/2014/11/06/home-depot-hackers-stolen-data/18613167/

CNET. (n.d.). Home Depot offers $19M to settle customers hacking lawsuit.

https://www.cnet.com/news/privacy/home-depot-offers-19m-to-settle-customers-hacking-lawsuit/

The New York Times. (2017, October 3). The Yahoo hack affected 3 billion users.

https://www.nytimes.com/2017/10/03/technology/yahoo-hack-3-billion-users.html

Wired. (n.d.). Under Armour MyFitnessPal hack.

https://www.wired.com/story/under-armour-myfitnesspal-hack-password-hashing/

CPO Magazine. (n.d.). Lessons from the Uber breach settlement.

https://www.cpomagazine.com/cyber-security/lessons-from-the-uber-breach-settlement/

The New York Times. (2018, November 30). Marriott data breach.

https://www.nytimes.com/2018/11/30/business/marriott-data-breach.html

CNN. (2019, July 29). Capital One data breach.

https://www.cnn.com/2019/07/29/business/capital-one-data-breach/

Wikipedia. (n.d.). 2020 Twitter account hijacking.

https://en.wikipedia.org/wiki/2020_Twitter_account_hijacking

Financial Times. (n.d.). SolarWinds breach.

https://www.ft.com/content/c13dbb51-907b-4db7-8347-30921ef931c2

TechCrunch. (2023, December 4). 23andMe confirms hackers stole ancestry data on 6.9 million users.

https://techcrunch.com/2023/12/04/23andme-confirms-hackers-stole-ancestry-data-on-6-9-million-users/

thank you

THANK YOU FOR READING MY BOOK

I really appreciate all of your feedback and I love hearing what you have to say.

I need your input to make the next version of this book and my future books better.

Please take two minutes now and leave a helpful review on Amazon letting me know what you thought of the book.

Thanks so much!

Sergey Poltev

MY GIFT TO YOU!

Congratulations on reading HACK PROOF!

As my Gift to you, get FREE Access to the Audiobook of HACK PROOF and other Free Resources by scanning the QR Code below or visiting HackProofBook.com

Made in the USA
Monee, IL
04 November 2026

67387311R00115